THE
LAIS OF
MARIE DE
FRANCE

BY
ROBERT W. HANNING

*The Vision of History in
Early Britain: from Gildas to
Geoffrey of Monmouth*

*The Individual in Twelfth
Century Romance*

BY
JOAN M. FERRANTE

*The Conflict of Love and
Honor: The medieval Tristan
legend in France, Germany,
and Italy*

(Translator.)
Guillaume d'Orange. *Four
Twelfth Century Epics*

Editor with George Economou.
*In Pursuit of Perfection:
Courtly Love in Medieval
Literature*

*Woman as Image in Medieval
Literature, from the Twelfth
Century to Dante*

The Lais of Marie de France

*Translated,
with an introduction
and notes, by*

ROBERT HANNING
& JOAN FERRANTE

THE LABYRINTH PRESS
Durham, North Carolina

For information contact:
The Labyrinth Press, P.O. Box 2124
Durham, N.C. 27702

Library of Congress Cataloging
in Publication Data

Marie, de France, 12th cent.
The lais of Marie de France.

Translation of: Lais.
Reprint. Originally published:
New York: Dutton, c1978.
Bibliography: p.
Contents:
Prologue—Guigemar—Equitan—{etc.}
I. Hanning, Robert W.
II. Ferrante, Joan M., 1936–.
III. Title.
{PQ1494.L3E5   1982}
841'.1   81–19278
ISBN 0–939464–02–0   AACR2

To
our
students

Contents

THE
LAIS OF
MARIE DE
FRANCE

✣ INTRODUCTION

MARIE DE FRANCE was perhaps the greatest woman author of
the Middle Ages and certainly the creator of the finest medieval
short fiction before Boccaccio and Chaucer. Her best work, the
Lais—the collection of short romances and tales translated in
this volume—is a major achievement of the first age of French
literature and of the "Renaissance of the Twelfth Century,"
that remarkable efflorescence of Western European culture
that signaled the end of the "Dark Ages" and the beginning
of many ideas and institutions basic to modern civilization.
One of the twelfth century's most significant innovations was
its rediscovery of love as a literary subject—a subject that it
depicted, anatomized, celebrated, and mocked in a series of
masterpieces, almost all of which were written in lucid French
verse. Among these pioneering love texts, which would soon
be adapted and imitated in all the vernaculars of Europe, none
better stands the test of time than Marie's *Lais*. The combina-
tion of variety, virtuosity, and economy of means that charac-
terizes the twelve short stories of fulfilled or frustrated passion
—the shortest of which, *Chevrefoil,* is but 118 lines long, while
the longest, *Eliduc,* requires but 1,184—gives ample and con-
stant evidence of Marie's mastery of plot, characterization, and
diction, while the woman's point of view she brings to her
material further distinguishes the *Lais* from the longer nar-
ratives of love and adventure composed by her male contem-
poraries, of whom the best known to modern readers is
Chrétien de Troyes, the creator of Arthurian romance and the
first chronicler of the love of Lancelot and Guinevere.

Unfortunately, we know practically nothing about this su-
perb storyteller, except for her name, her extant works (in
addition to the *Lais,* a collection of animal fables and the moral,
supernatural tale, *St. Patrick's Purgatory*), the approximate
period of her literary activities (1160?–1215?), and the fact,
derived from her name and comments in her writings, that
she was of French birth but wrote at or for the English court,

I

which, as a result of the Norman Conquest, was French-speaking in her days. (See below for further information about Marie's activities and other works.) From the *Lais*, however, a comprehensive picture of Marie's artistic personality and predilections emerges, several facets of which deserve particular attention.

Perhaps the most recognizable "signature" of her work is the symbolic creature or artifact around which a *lai* is organized for maximum intensity and suggestiveness within the least possible narrative duration. The nightingale in *Laüstic*, the hazel tree wound about with honeysuckle in *Chevrefoil*, the hungry swan in *Milun*—all provide valuable insight into the nature of love in their respective narratives, insight that might otherwise require development through thousands of lines of poetry. Marie carefully places her symbols in the context of character revelation and tersely expressed dramatic irony, which prompts the reader to draw separate conclusions about the worth of the lovers and their love in a given *lai*. Accordingly, symbols and situations frequently parallel each other in two or more *lais*, yet the denouements, and the judgments we pass on their justice or injustice, will vary widely from one *lai* to another. The result of this process of "paired contrasts" is that, as we read on, our experience of each narrative is reinforced and complicated by resonances, often ironic, of its predecessors. What emerges is not a unified moral perspective on passion and its consequences: Marie's art avoids easy generalizations such as "married love is wrong, adultery right," or the reverse, but demonstrates instead that character, fortune, and the ability to seize and manipulate opportunities interact in any love relationship. Devotion, loyalty, ingenuity, which transcend marital ties or social norms, provide the grounds for our sympathies with or condemnation of any of Marie's lovers.

In addition to our involvement with the protagonists of the *Lais*, we respond constantly to the mastery with which Marie presents them. The deft touches of irony (as in the conclusion of *Equitan*, where the adulterous king, to avoid discovery, leaps into the vat of boiling water he has prepared in order to destroy his mistress's husband), or of homely sentiment (e.g., the description of the early-morning discovery of the abandoned infant heroine of *Le Fresne* by the porter of a monastery), remind us of the artist's complete control across the entire spectrum of narrative technique. Marie tells us in the *Prologue* to the *Lais* that she has undertaken the novel task of translating the body of love tales created by the Bretons, those famous exponents of the art of exotic storytelling. As there are no extant "Breton *lais*," we cannot substantiate Marie's claim or decide to what extent her plots may follow Breton originals. But it is clear from her use of classical Latin and contemporaneous French material that she was a well-educated and highly trained literary craftsman who wished to be recognized for her skills. She wrote as an expert on love and storytelling for the first large, sophisticated, and elite audience of medieval Europe—an audience that appreciated, as we can, the inventiveness as well as the charm and power of her love tales. In order to appreciate Marie's achievement fully, the modern reader should know something of the cultural milieu in which she worked.

The twelfth century in Western Europe saw a tremendous expansion of intellectual, social, and artistic activity; it was truly a cultural renaissance, responding to new political structures, social tensions, and economic advances that were only dimly foreshadowed during the early-medieval centuries. The expansion of urban life brought with it the rise of scholastic centers, which were usually attached to the cathedrals of important towns like Chartres and Paris. Training in grammar (or, as we should call it, literary analysis and philology), rhetoric, and dialectic or logic produced a new class of intellectuals who were technically clerics but were often only minimally involved with or controlled by ecclesiastical authority, unlike their early-medieval predecessors, who were almost all monks and deeply committed to a life of religious observance and obedience. Graduates of the twelfth-century schools were equipped for service at the burgeoning courts of France and England, where they formed a civil service and also found an outlet for their literary abilities. The rise of a courtly aristocracy at these same centers of political power gave the school-trained *clercs* an audience that was also new in medieval civilization. It comprised, in addition to the learned clerics themselves, the greater and lesser aristocracy of *chevaliers,* who fought for a living but also cultivated arts of nonlethal competition and personal refinement that were unknown to early-medieval warriors; and—most important, in the opinion of many scholars— it also included noblewomen, many of whom were involved in feudal politics and highly educated in religious and secular subjects, even though regular courses of advanced study in the schools were open only to men. (Among the many remarkable women of the twelfth century, besides Marie, special recognition is due to Eleanor of Aquitaine, heiress to a great duchy and successively wife to the kings of France and England; her daughter Marie, Countess of Champagne and patroness of Chrétien de Troyes; and Héloïse, mistress and later wife of Peter Abélard, well known throughout France for her brilliance, courage, and successful career as an abbess.) The fertile interaction of these groups gave birth to a vernacular literature in which learned interests, previously expressed exclusively in Latin, and themes of importance to a courtly elite in search of self-defining ideals mingled and cross-pollinated.

One of the themes explored in twelfth-century courtly narrative was the individual's recognition of a need for self-fulfillment and his or her struggle for the freedom to satisfy this need. The tension between the personal quest for perfection and one's social obligations was a recurring theme of courtly literature, and narrative and lyric poets alike used love as a symbol of the quintessentially private sphere of existence and desire. The nature and problems of love—for it was by no means always viewed as a positive force by Marie and her contemporaries—were explored in lyrics and in long and short narratives. Besides Marie's *Lais,* the latter group includes *contes,* short tales borrowed from the works of Ovid, the classical master of love and self-conscious art, whose influence was everywhere visible in the period. Among authors of longer chivalric romances, Chrétien de Troyes dominates the age, but Béroul and Thomas, authors of versions of the tragic love story of Tristan and Isolt, and Gautier d'Arras also excelled. All explored the problematic interrelationship of love and chivalry from many points of view, with an art that moved easily from quasi-symbolic representation to detached social comedy.

The narratives of the courtly poets were connoisseurs' literature: fanciful, ingenious tales that simultaneously amused their audience and challenged it to discover deeper meanings beneath the polished language and the idealized adventures. A long chivalric romance of Chrétien, for example, comprises a series of puzzles to be solved by aficionados of the genre: Why did the hero or heroine act in a particular, unexpected way at a particular moment? What vice or anti-courtly attitude does a villain represent? Unlike earlier medieval epics, in which heroic values are universally acknowledged even though cowardice or treachery may cause their subversion, twelfth-century courtly tales and romances usually portray the protagonist's gradual discovery of real values through love (one thinks of Marie's Guigemar, for whom love is wounding and healing, a cause of sorrow before it is a cause of joy), or the transformation of a delusory set of external appearances and relationships by the timely revelation of a hero or heroine's true identity (as is the case in *Le Fresne*). The line of European narrative fiction that uses the portrayal of love as a means for exploring the interaction of self and society, appearance and reality, descends continuously from the twelfth-century courtly narrative to the twentieth-century novel. Marie is thus one of the creators—the only woman among them—of a grand tradition that has shaped and defined our literary culture.

We know almost nothing about Marie herself, except that she was originally French and lived in the latter part of the twelfth century. It is not unusual to have virtually no information about medieval authors except what we can glean from their and others' works. There are none of the public records and reactions we take so for granted with modern writers—

no copyrights or publication dates, no standard editions, no critical reviews, no authors' memoirs or letters to establish the date or proper text of a work. More often than not, the best manuscripts we have are much later than the works themselves and have gone through several copyings; if there is more than one manuscript, they usually do not agree in all particulars. All of this means that we have to learn mainly by inference, to establish the text by judicious comparison and selection, and to deduce facts about the author from references in the work, from connections with the works of others (when there are obvious sources or influences), and, though much more rarely, from direct remarks by other writers, as in Gottfried's literary excursus in the *Tristan.*

All we know about Marie besides her name is her work: the *Lais,* the *Fables,* and *St. Patrick's Purgatory* (*L'Espurgatoire Saint Patrice*).[1] Marie names herself at the beginning of the first *lai,* at the end of the *Purgatory,* and at the end of the *Fables,* in the latter case rather assertively:

> Me numerai pur remembrance
> Marie ai nun, si sui de France.
> Put cel estre que clerc plusur
> prendreient sur eus mun labur,
> ne voil que sur li le die.

> I shall name myself so that it will be remembered;
> Marie is my name, I am of France.
> It may be that many clerks
> will take my labor on themselves.
> I don't want any of them to claim it.

"De France" means, presumably, that she was born in France, either the Continent as opposed to England or the Ile de France as opposed to Occitaine, probably not that she was of the royal house (as some have assumed).[2] Beyond that, she tells us only that she wrote the *Lais* for a "noble king" and the *Fables* for a Count William. The king is probably Henry II (ruled 1154–89).[3] Count William may be William Longsword (Guillaume Longespée), illegitimate son of Henry II, Count of Salisbury after about 1197, or William Marshall, Earl of Pembroke from 1199, or William of Gloucester, or, most likely of all, William of Mandeville,[4] Earl of Essex from 1167 (died 1189).

Marie herself is even more difficult to identify. She may be the illegitimate daughter of Geoffrey of Anjou—and hence a sister of Henry II—who became abbess of Shaftesbury around 1181 and died c. 1216, or the abbess of Reading, or Marie de Meulan, daughter of Count Waleran de Beaumont.[5] It seems unlikely that we shall ever really know who she was. All we can be sure of is that she frequented the court of Henry II and Eleanor, that she was probably a noblewoman (the circle in which she moved, the subjects that concerned her, and the level of her education make it extremely unlikely that she was not of noble birth—a lower-class laywoman would have had little opportunity for education). She was certainly educated, knowing, besides her native French, Latin, from which she translated the *Purgatory,* and English, from which she translated the *Fables.* But even her dates are difficult to determine. If we accept the chronological order of *Lais, Fables, Purgatory,*[6] we are still left with a wide range of years. The *Purgatory* was probably written after 1189 because it mentions a Saint Malachi (l. 2074), who was not canonized until 1189; it may have been done as late as 1208–15.[7] The *Lais* have been dated from 1155–70, by analogy with other literary works that seem to have influenced Marie: Wace's *Brut,* c. 1155, *Piramus et Tisbé,* 1155–60, and *Éneas,* c. 1160.[8] Several critics think that Chrétien knew Marie's *Prologue,* which she wrote after the *Lais,* by the time he wrote *Erec;*[9] if this is so, the *Lais* were probably written by 1170.

We can make such connèctions with other literary works, but they do not help us with the dating, since we cannot date the analogous works precisely. *Eliduc* was probably a source for Gautier d'Arras's *Ille et Galeron,* dated 1178–85.[10] Denis Piramus mentions Marie's *Lais* in his *Vie S. Edmund le Rei,* saying that they are popular among counts, barons, knights, and ladies (11.35-48); if Denis wrote between 1170 and 1180, as his editor, Kjellman, thinks, the *Lais* must have been written by then. Certainly Marie knew some version of the Tristan legend (she tells part of the story in the *Chevrefoil* and seems to use episodes in other *lais:* the procession of lovely ladies, each mistaken in turn for the heroine, in *Lanval;* the trap of stakes set for the lover in *Yonec;* the secret shrine of love in the woods in *Eliduc*); but whether she knew the Tristan poems that we have—Béroul, Thomas, or some earlier version —we cannot tell.[11] We can only say that Marie probably wrote the *Lais* between 1160 and 1199.[12]

She wrote them all in French, in octosyllabic couplets. For the *Lais*, she drew on Celtic tales, probably oral, and French sources, in some cases written. She seems to have known Ovid and contemporary versions of other classical material, like Wace's *Brut*, the *Roman de Thèbes*, and the *Roman d'Éneas*, as well as Arthurian tales and the Tristan story. The *Fables* draw on at least two versions of the *Romulus*, derived from a Latin version of Aesop; the *Roman de Renart* material; popular tales; and *fabliaux*. The *Purgatory* is a translation of a Latin text, *Tractatus de Purgatori sancti Patricii*, by the monk Henry of Saltrey.

Marie begins the *Fables*, as she does the *Lais*, with a conventional prologue that reveals her sense of moral obligation: those who know letters should give their attention to the books and words of philosophers, who wrote down moral precepts so that others might improve themselves. This didactic purpose is not absent from any of Marie's material. She has translated the *Fables*, she tells us in the epilogue, from English into French as Alfred had translated them from Latin into English, and as Aesop did from Greek into Latin (a popular belief). They are short tales with a moral lesson at the end, using, for the most part, animals as the principal actors, in the Aesopic tradition. The lessons are conventional: the dangers of greed and pride, the oppression of the weak by the strong, the superiority of a simple life over a luxurious one lived in servitude or terror—the *Lais* make many of the same points, but in a far more subtle way. Marie gives several of the *Fables* a feudal twist with the lessons she draws from them: xxvii, a man cannot have honor if he shames his lord, nor can a lord have honor if he shames his men; xix, those who choose bad lords are foolish, for by subjecting themselves to cruel and evil men they gain nothing but shame; lxii, a prince should not have a covetous or deceptive seneschal in his kingdom unless he wants to make him his lord. Some of these lessons are of interest in connection with a recurring theme in Marie's *Lais*— the journey to another land and a new life: ci, no one should put himself in the hands of one who would harm him: rather, he should go to another land; xxii, if you look for a better land, you never find one where you will be without fear or sorrow; lxxx, those who do ill in their own country and depart leave it to no purpose, because they will do the same wherever they go; it is their hearts they should change rather than their countries. This is, indeed, what several of Marie's heroes do.[13]

In *Saint Patrick's Purgatory,* the hero makes a spiritual journey to another land, from which he returns a better Christian. This work, which Marie translated from Latin, has a religious as well as a moral purpose: it was intended not only to help others to improve themselves, but also to teach them to fear and serve God. At the same time, although the subject is overtly otherworldly—the pains of purgatory and the joys of the earthly paradise as seen by an Irish knight—one cannot help, once again, making connections with the *Lais*. The journey through purgatory is described as if it were real, but the narrative is preceded by a comment that suggests it is actually a vision: many souls, we are told, leave their bodies temporarily, have visions or revelations, and then return; they see in the spirit what seems to be corporeal, and they only *seem* to feel the real pains (ll. 163ff.). (One wonders if this is what happens to those characters in the *Lais* who apparently have strange, otherworldly adventures—e.g., in *Guigemar, Lanval,* and *Yonec,* people are transported by magic by the will of those who desire them; it is perhaps only the spirit that goes, and yet the body seems to have the experience.) The Irish knight, after he has repented his sins, approaches purgatory through a deep hole in the earth, following a long, dark passage that finally opens onto a field, where he sees a beautiful house (cf. the tunnel through the hill, then the meadow, and finally the bird-knight's castle in *Yonec*). In the house, monks prepare the knight for the journey he is about to undertake, and for the temptations and torments of the devils he will encounter. He passes through them all—and they are described in graphic and grotesque detail—calling continually on God to defend him. Finally he crosses a bridge that leads to a land of light, where a religious procession welcomes him with joy; the Irish knight may expect to return to this place after he dies, and after he has actually experienced the torments he just witnessed. This paradise, where souls go when they are delivered from the pains of purgatory, is on this earth, in the East; here they will remain until the Last Judgment, when they will go to heaven. It may be the same sort of earthly paradise that Marie has in mind, in the *Lais*, as the homeland of the fairy in *Lanval*, or of the bird-knight in *Yonec*. Her heroes or heroines can experience the joy of such a place only briefly, only as momentary visions, in this life, but that is often enough to sustain them. Lanval alone chooses to relinquish this world and follow his love back to her otherworld; the lady in *Yonec* makes her way to such a land, but is not permitted to remain.

The *Lais* are the one work for which Marie does not claim a literary source. They are tales she has heard and put into rhyme: Celtic tales, which were originally transmitted by Breton minstrels, but whether Marie heard them in French or in Celtic is not altogether clear. She does give some of the names in "Bretan" (*Bisclavret*, l. 3; *Lanval*, l. 4; *Laüstic*, ll. 2-4), which suggests that she knows something of the language, but since she also gives the meaning of some names in English, we cannot assume on that basis that her direct source was Celtic. In any case, she makes it clear that she is the first to put these stories into rhyme, that is, into a conventional literary form, the octosyllabic couplet. She is not the first to render short narratives in verse (the Ovidian tales, *Narcissus* and *Piramus et Tisbé,* antedate the *Lais*), but she may be the first to do it with nonclassical material.

Courtly romances in Marie's period treat Celtic subjects in narrative poems, but they are much longer than Marie's *Lais.* The romances also differ from the *Lais* in that they are concerned with both love and chivalry, with the proper balance between a knight's responsibility to his society, his service to others, and the fulfillment of his own desires while Marie's primary concern is with the personal needs of the knight or—and this is unique in this literature—of the lady. In her *Lais,* the lovers often live in a hostile world—a court that rejects, a marriage that enslaves, social conventions that constrain—and love offers the only opportunity to escape that world; to free the mind, if not the body, from the world's oppression; to endure the pains. This is not to say that every *lai* presents a picture of an ideal love; several (*Equitan, Bisclavret, Laüstic, Chaitivel*) reveal the treachery or selfishness of imperfect love. In fact, as many critics have pointed out, the *Lais* offer a spectrum of love situations.[14] If one goes systematically through the collection, noting the aspect of love that Marie emphasizes in each, one ends with a fairly complete sense of her idea of love, as well as the strong impression that she conceived of the *lais* as complementary pieces.[15] We cannot be sure that the order we follow is the order Marie intended. It is, however, the order given in manuscript (H), which is the earliest extant manuscript, the only one that contains all twelve *Lais,* the one and widely accepted as the best available version; but H is mid-thirteenth-century, not contemporary, and therefore may not reflect the author's plan. Bearing this reservation about the order of the *Lais* in mind, we can nonetheless note obvious correspondences among them, opposing perspectives and variations on the same theme.

The message in the early *lais* seems fairly clear, but as we read further into the collection, and as they resonate more and more with each other, the moral line becomes more ambiguous, more complicated. The first two *lais* (Marie does tell us in so many words that she is beginning with *Guigemar*) offer a fairly straightforward contrast between fulfilling and destructive love. Guigemar is a good knight who lacks only love, which is symbolized by his wound; his lady, trapped in an unhappy marriage with a possessive old man, also lacks love. Guigemar's love frees and fulfills her, her love cures and fulfills him. Neither chivalry nor marriage can function properly without love (in *Milun*, Marie will show how chivalry can interfere with love and marriage). *Guigemar* focuses on the needs of the hero and on the bond between the lovers; there is no relationship, no trust to be broken, between the woman's husband and the hero, and the husband's claims on his wife are undercut by his treatment of her. The love is thus virtually without stain (if somewhat limited in comparison to what we see of love in the last *lais*), as the aid and sanction of supernatural forces suggest. In *Equitan*, the second *lai*, there *is* a bond between the two men (the husband and the lover) that is both personal and public—the husband is the lover's seneschal and serves him loyally, so the king's affair with his wife is at once self-indulgence and a betrayal of a public trust. The wife's moral position is not justified because of any mistreatment; indeed, it is vitiated by her husband's goodness and her possessiveness and ambition. There is no supernatural intervention; on the contrary, the machinations of the lovers are responsible for all that happens. One concludes that, important as love is in the fulfillment of the individual, it is not to be pursued at all costs. The different natures of these two loves—one necessary and true, and ultimately rewarded; the other self-indulgent and treacherous, and finally punished —are pointed up by the ease with which the first is acknowledged (a woman with a good sense of her own and her lover's worth, Guigemar says, need not be begged at length [ll. 513ff.]), while Equitan has to carry on a lengthy debate, filled with ironies, in order to persuade his lady to love him— as if the more words, the less feeling.[16]

Guigemar shows how necessary love is, and how real love can endure the proofs of suffering and separation; *Equitan* shows how a love that arises solely for pleasure, from self-indulgence rather than deep need, can lead to treachery and self-destruction. In the third *lai, Le Fresne,* a love that begins as simple pleasure and physical indulgence rises, through the woman's devotion, to self-sacrifice, which ultimately earns its reward. But in *Bisclavret,* the *lai* which follows *Le Fresne,* the woman cannot attain the degree of devotion her situation requires; instead, fearing for her own safety and unmoved by her husband's suffering, she betrays him and is punished for it. The devotion Fresne shows to her lover, despite his willingness to bow to social pressures and marry another woman, is eventually repaid, not simply by marriage to him, but by reunion with her parents and sister, and a recovery of her identity. Bisclavret's wife, who faces an equally demanding test, fails to pass it. She betrays her husband's love and trust, turns to another man, and incurs lasting shame for herself and her descendants. Bisclavret, like Fresne, lives many years in exile from his true self (Bisclavret as a werewolf, Fresne as a foundling); both had been rejected by women who failed in their family responsibilities, in the first case, that of a wife to her husband, and in the second, that of a mother to her child; both are protected in their defenseless states: Fresne by the abbess who takes her in, Bisclavret by his king, who rescues and sustains him. Marie has extended the scope of her attention to significant human relations beyond the pair of lovers (the family, and the court). The king in *Bisclavret* rewards the loyalty of a good vassal, whom he does not recognize but whose gesture of devotion he appreciates, in contrast to the king Equitan, who abused the loyalty of a faithful minister; in both *Bisclavret* and *Equitan,* the wronged husband is avenged on his wife and survives, a nice balance to the defeat or destruction of the unsympathetically treated husbands in *Guigemar, Yonec,* and *Milun.*

Indeed, Marie attempts to balance her presentations to a

remarkable degree. In the first four *lais*, she seems to be concerned with a sexual balance: a good pair of lovers in *Guigemar*, a bad pair in *Equitan*, a woman's devotion in *Le Fresne*, a man's endurance in *Bisclavret*; a deficient husband and a poor king in *Guigemar* and *Equitan*, a bad mother and treacherous wife in *Le Fresne* and *Bisclavret*; a wise and kind abbess in *Le Fresne*, a sensitive and wise counselor in *Bisclavret*. There is a similar balance in the next pair of *lais*: a knight caught in the trap of a society that refuses to recognize his worth (*Lanval*), a princess imprisoned by the possessive love of a father who will not allow her to marry (*Les Deus Amanz*); both are rescued by a love that is put to public trial, which turns out well in one case, sadly in the other. In both *lais*, there is a king hindered in his public duty by personal ties: in *Lanval*, by subservience to an immoral and vindictive wife, in *Les Deus Amanz*, by possessive attachment to a child.

Although, by subjecting it to public trials, Marie further extends the public aspect of the love in *Lanval* and *Les Deus Amanz* and thus continues the move outwards she made in *Le Fresne* and *Bisclavret* by introducing significant relationships outside the pair of lovers, she ultimately rejects the public setting: both Lanval and the girl in *Deus Amanz* leave their societies in order to follow their loves. Lanval exonerates himself before his court and retains his love because he is able to make a total commitment to that love, which had given him all that the world denied him—wealth, success, and joy—to the extent that he even leaves his world behind to follow it (her) to an unknown world. The girl in *Les Deus Amanz* is unwilling to leave her father and commit herself completely to her love, and therefore she loses her love. But her lover is also at fault: love inspired him with a feeling of unusual strength, with a belief that he could overcome any obstacle, but it also makes him so impatient and reckless that he refuses the help he needs, his strength fails, and he dies. He makes a total commitment in his effort to win the girl, but he refuses the aid she has provided, whereas Lanval graciously accepts all the fairy offers. Marie seems to be saying that one must not only serve love with total devotion, as in *Le Fresne,* but also be ready to receive what love gives.

The source of help in *Lanval* is supernatural, a fairy's powers; in *Les Deus Amanz,* it is the human knowledge and skill of the Salerno doctor (another woman). Marie alternates supernatural force with human ingenuity throughout the *lais;* the supernatural is usually positive or helpful to the lovers (as in *Guigemar* [I], *Lanval* [V], *Yonec* [VII]), while the human is usually treacherous or destructive (as in *Equitan* [II], *Les Deus Amanz* [VI], and *Laustic* [VIII]). Always maintaining her sense of balance, Marie reverses the situation in *Le Fresne* (III) and *Bisclavret* (IV).

There is another kind of alternation at work in *Lanval* and *Les Deus Amanz*—between a love that is taken seriously (*Lanval*) and a love that has comic or parodistic overtones (*Les Deus Amanz*). The same is true of the next pair: the love in *Yonec* is serious and tragic; the love in *Laustic* is superficial and frustrated. The former, however, is fruitful, while the latter issues only in a dead symbol. In both *Laustic* and *Les Deus Amanz* the lovers play at love; in *Les Deus Amanz,* they fail because they don't really understand the game, and in *Laustic,* they only go through the motions without real feeling.

Yonec and *Laustic* return to the love situation of the first *lais* in the collection, the triangle: as in *Guigemar,* there is an unhappy marriage in *Yonec,* with a lover coming magically from afar; in *Laustic,* as in *Equitan,* there is a self-indulgent affair in which the lover is bound by friendship to the husband. In this set of *lais,* however, the husband is a much more active figure and his action introduces considerable violence into the two stories. The lover in *Yonec,* who appears in the form of a bird, is killed in a vicious trap laid by the husband, who is himself killed, many years later, by the lover's son—violence begets violence; in *Laustic,* the bird, which symbolizes the love is killed viciously by the husband. In *Yonec*, the lover leaves a trail of blood which his lady follows; in *Laustic*, the bird's blood stains the lady's gown. In both *lais*, the husband is a hunter, a predator, and the lovers are his victims; and in both, it is the joy felt by the lady that makes her husband aware of her love and arouses his desire to destroy it. Marie is saying that love does not exist in a vacuum, that even a good love is vulnerable to the hostility of the world around it. In *Laustic*, however, the lady's joy is superficial, represented by the feigned delight in the nightingale's song; the love is nothing more than an exchange of gifts and words, and at the first threat of danger, the attack on the bird, both lovers give it up, relegating it to the symbol of the dead bird in an ornate coffin. Theirs is a stillborn love, with no issue, while the love in *Yonec*, though it ends tragically for the lover, does not die with him; the bird-knight is killed, but his child lives to avenge him. Thus, as in *Guigemar*, because the need for love is real and the love good, it cannot be completely destroyed by the hostile world. The world around the lovers seems to become more and more of an obstacle or a threat in these *lais;* but at the same time, the love, when it is good, lasts and is fruitful.

In *Milun*, the *lai* that follows *Yonec* and *Laustic* and is thematically linked to them by the motif of a bird (in this case a messenger of love), a child is also born of the love; he grows up not to avenge his father, but to meet him in combat, and to reunite him with his mother. The *lais* that present negative aspects of love do not extend over a long period of time, indicating perhaps that the situations they describe, of self-indulgent or superficial feeling, are static, while in the other *lais* the love is active and aids the individual to grow. The time span in the *lais* which present positive aspects of love seems, in contrast, to increase through the collection: in the first, *Guigemar*, we see a lover grow from an unfeeling adolescent to a loving adult; in *Le Fresne*, the heroine grows from a foundling to a loving woman; in *Yonec*, a child is born and grows up to avenge his father; in *Milun*, the child grows up to reunite his long-separated parents. Actually, in *Milun*, the peacefully resolved combat with the father indicates that the father has finally grown up. Chivalry must, as it were, defeat itself before love can function fully.

Milun, and the *lai* that follows it, *Chaitivel*, are both concerned with fighting for glory and the relation between chivalry and love, which is normally a romance subject, but not treated here as it would be in a romance. Marie does not seek a balance between chivalry and love, but shows instead how chivalry—when it means only the pursuit of worldly glory—interferes with love, seriously in *Milun*, humorously in *Chaitivel* (again that balance). In *Milun*, all the characters (father, mother, and son) are caught up in the pursuit of glory—glory is what first attracts the girl to the knight, what separates them, and what finally brings the father and the son together when both become rivals for the same reputation. It is only the son's compassion for his father's white hair that prevents serious tragedy; human feeling in the issue of the love finally defeats the desire for glory that had for so long stood in its way.

There is, however, another element at work in the *lai*, which counters the violence of fighting—the written word. When the lovers cannot be together, they correspond for twenty years. We are moving, here, toward a higher level of understanding between lovers, a communication of thought which serves when physical consummation is impossible (cf. Tristan and Isolt in *Chevrefoil*). That words are meant to replace physical force is underscored by the arrival of a letter announcing the death of the mother's husband just as the son prepares to go and kill him. The same opposition between words and arms is presented in *Chaitivel*: the four lovers attempt to win the lady's love by fighting, but they try too hard; three of them are killed and the fourth incapacitated. The lady, who glories in their devotion, attempts to comfort the remaining lover with her conversation, and assuages her own grief by composing a poem about it. The whole *lai* reveals the foolishness of literary conventions of love—indeed, both *lais, Milun* and *Chaitivel,* expose the futility of the romantic view of knightly service for love.

In the following *lai,* the *Chevrefoil,* unsatisfied love is again the inspiration for a poem, but in this case, the lover transcends his sorrow at the enforced separation by writing a *lai* that records the joy he experienced when the lovers were together. He transforms love to art in his *lai* as Marie does in hers. Tristan and Isolt are able to meet for only a brief moment— the rest of their life is bitter pain—but they manage to derive great joy from the words they exchange, which is all they can hope for in this life. In *Eliduc,* too, though the lovers by mutual consent renounce the world in order to give their lives to God, words remain their one point of contact; they send messages back and forth and offer prayers to God for each other, a higher form, perhaps, of the *lai* in which Tristan records his love, but not unrelated. In the last four *lais* of the collection, the word seems to replace supernatural forces and human ingenuity (which alternately dominated the earlier *lais*) as the symbol or expression of the love Marie is describing. The spirit of the love, freed from physical and worldly concerns, is conveyed by the characters' words, as it is by Marie's poetry. Magic symbolized their feelings, words express them. The ability to commit the feelings to words indicates a control, perhaps even a transcendence, of them.

The separation of the lovers in *Milun,* dictated by the demands of the world, of chivalry and marriage, lasts twenty years: in *Chaitivel,* the separation, forced by death and physical disability, is final; in *Chevrefoil,* the separation is caused by social pressures of the woman's marriage, as in *Milun,* but further complicated by Tristan's relation to her husband, and it is lifelong, broken only by brief encounters. The separation in the last *lai, Eliduc,* is brought about by renunciation. First the wife renounces her husband and her worldly life, and then the lovers renounce their marriage and the world; all three make their sacrifices in favor of a higher love. Paradoxically, however, their renunciation of the physical union and of the world draws them all closer together in a selfless love. This *lai,* which centers like so many others on a love triangle, resolves the problem in a unique way, by rearranging the three characters in three successive pairings, ending with the two women living together as sisters in a convent. This *lai,* which is the longest, also resolves various earlier themes: the knight wronged by his king, as in *Lanval,* is vindicated and restored; in exile he fights, not for his own glory, but to defend another king from attack; nature, not magic or human ingenuity, offers the means to revive the princess. At the same time, *Eliduc* presents complicated human situations, which cannot easily be resolved: we are not allowed the simple expedient of a vicious spouse to enable us to sympathize with the lovers; the two women, the devoted wife and the naïve girl, both command our sympathy. Even the knight, who is weak, indulgent, and sometimes violent in his pursuit of the new love, cannot simply be condemned—he is wrongly exiled, but serves both his own and his adopted lands well, and falls naturally enough into a relationship that offers him human comfort (something we have been taught to applaud in other *lais*). As in *Chevrefoil,* we are forced to acknowledge the demands and pressures of society, of knightly service and marriage, even when they conflict with love. Yet even here Marie does not insist on a total renunciation of human love—how could she when she has been at such pains to teach its values and show its positive effects?—but she does offer other possibilities when physical satisfaction is impossible: art and religious devotion.

In the course of the *lais,* Marie presents a realistic picture of human love despite, or perhaps partly by means of, the supernatural trappings.[17] Love offers joy, but never altogether without pain, and regardless of its strength, it cannot last forever. Note how often death intervenes, particularly in the later *lais: Les Deus Amanz, Yonec, Laustic, Chaitivel;* in *Equitan* the lovers also die, albeit deservedly; in *Chevrefoil* their death is forecast; and in *Lanval* and *Eliduc* they move into another life. Throughout the *lais,* the world—in the shape of jealous husbands, possessive fathers, selfish wives or mothers, ungrateful lords—seems hostile to the lovers. Often it imprisons them: the wives in *Guigemar* and *Yonec* in towers; the wife in *Laustic* in her house; the women in *Milun* and *Chevrefoil* in their marriages; the man in *Bisclavret* in his wolf form; the girl in *Eliduc* in a deathlike trance; the girl in *Les Deus Amanz* by the impossible task her father sets her suitors. The lovers are exiled, outcast, rejected: Guigemar, because of his wound, becomes a stranger in a foreign land; Fresne is rejected first by her mother, who abandons her to strangers, and later by her lover; Bisclavret as a werewolf is shut out of human society; the court ostracized Lanval and he, in turn, rejects it; the lover in *Yonec* is a stranger from another land, the lady an outsider in his; Milun exiles himself from his love in order to pursue glory; in *Chaitivel*, death permanently exiles three of the lovers; Tristan lives in permanent exile; Eliduc, banished by his king at the beginning of the *lai*, exiles himself from the world at the end.

Exile necessitates a journey to another land, sometimes another world, and Marie seems to imply that love *is* ultimately of another world.[18] It may sometimes bring freedom to those who are confined, as it does to the women in *Guigemar* and in *Yonec*—they are able to leave their towers without difficulty when they decide to follow their love—but it cannot survive being constrained within a small space, as in *Laustic*.[19] It must have some issue—if not a child, as in *Yonec* and *Milun*, then a symbol, such as the flowers in *Les Deus Amanz* or the enshrined bird in *Laustic*, which represent loves that, for different reasons, never fully lived; or poetry, whether the vain affirmation of the lady's triumph in *Chaitivel*, or the living recollection of real joy in *Chevrefoil*.

Marie develops her ideas not by direct statement but through symbols, by emphasizing small but significant details.[20] The genre she chose to write in, the *lai*, because it is so much shorter than the romance, the other available narrative form for similar subjects, necessitates the focus on details. The first clue she gives us to the meaning of a *lai* is often its title, about which she makes a considerable fuss, sometimes giving alternatives, as in *Chaitivel,* where the two names indicate two perspectives: the lady's (she wants to call it *Quatre Dols,* the *Four Sorrows,* to commemorate all her admirers), and the man's (he insists on *Chaitivel,* the *Unfortunate One,* meaning himself). The last *lai* also has two names; formerly *Eliduc,* it is now known as *Guildeluec and Gualadun:* that is, for Marie it is more the story of the two women than of the man. Sometimes a name makes an ironic comment on the story, as in *Equitan* and perhaps *Le Fresne* (Equitan lowers himself, improperly, to a position of equality with his seneschal by making love to the latter's wife and leaving the seneschal to run the kingdom; Fresne, the ash tree, suggests a whole range of nurture and abandonment—see the comments on the *lai,* p. 90.)[21] For some *lais,* Marie supplies the title in several languages, as though to point up the universality of the situation (*Bisclavret, Laustic, Chevrefoil*). In some cases, the name serves as a symbol of the love: Laustic is the nightingale, dead but richly preserved; in *Chevrefoil,* the honeysuckle evokes the two lives bound together; Yonec is the child born of the love. In *Les Deus Amanz,* as in *Chaitivel,* the lovers are not named, but Marie makes much of the names of the places where the story occurs, suggesting that the lovers are, in effect, dominated by the world around them, which eventually overwhelms them. Marie makes it a point to recall the name of each *lai,* usually at its end. She reminds us, both at the beginning and at the end of most of the *lais,* that they are stories she has heard and recast: that is, she never lets us forget that she is the intermediary between us and the material. It is not unusual for medieval writers to call attention to themselves and to the authority of their versions (cf. Gottfried in *Tristan,* Wolfram in *Parzivàl*), because for the most part they were dealing with material that existed in other versions, and they were anxious to have their audience appreciate what they had brought to it.

In addition to its title, the symbolic object that is central to the narrative is often an indication of a *lai*'s meaning. The knot and belt which the lovers exchange in *Guigemar* represent the deep feeling and constancy of their love, a commitment that will endure for having been so freely given. It is significant that they do not exchange the conventional token of constancy, a ring, for Marie often uses rings ironically: in *Equitan,* the lovers exchange this standard symbol of loyalty while plotting to betray two loyalties, one to a husband, the other to a vassal; in *Le Fresne,* the ring the mother bestows on her abandoned child is a reminder of the bond that she denied; in *Milun, Chaitivel,* and *Eliduc,* the ring is the first token of love, the first sign of attraction and interest, but, as it happens, not necessarily of lasting devotion; and in *Eliduc,* the man's acceptance of a ring constitutes a denial of his marriage bond. In *Yonec,* the dying lover gives his lady a ring with the power to make her husband forget what has happened—scarcely a symbol of loyalty, however sympathetic we may be to the love.

In three successive *lais,* birds offer a symbolic comment on a love relationship: in *Yonec,* the lover appears in the form of a hawk; in *Laustic,* a live nightingale stands for the lover (in the lady's excuse to her husband), the dead bird, a lifeless object in a rich shrine, stands for the love; in *Milun,* a starving swan is the messenger of love, carrying letters between the lovers for twenty years. In both *Yonec* and *Milun,* the bird symbol gives way to a child, who, in *Yonec,* is all that remains of the union; while in *Milun* the child becomes the agent that reunites the lovers. The love in *Laustic* lacked the substance—not the opportunity, for in Marie will creates opportunity—to bear fruit, so its lifeless symbol is fittingly worshiped as though it had value.

The honeysuckle, which winds itself around the hazel so that neither can exist alone, just as Tristan and Isolt are bound together by their love, is the dominant symbol of *Chevrefoil;* one wonders what connection there is between the hazel of the metaphor in *Chevrefoil* and the names of the twins, Ash and Hazel, in *Le Fresne.* Marie does not mention the love potion which plays such an important part in other versions of the Tristan story, but she does use a potion in *Les Deus*

Amanz, not to arouse love or passion but to strengthen the love that already exists, and to enable it both to meet the challenges it faces and to bear fruit; since it is never drunk by the hero, the only fruit it produces are the flowers that grow where it spilled. It is tempting to see this potion as a comment on the Tristan story, perhaps even as an anti-potion.

A final important symbol is the hunt, an activity at once opposed to and emblematic of the love quest. Guigemar's hunting results in a self-inflicted wound that only a woman—his future mistress—can cure; Equitan avoids his public responsibility by hunting in the forest and violates feudal loyalty by "hunting" his seneschal's wife. Bisclavret has a pivotal hunting scene with the hero as the prey, while in *Yonec* the husband sets a trap for the bird-knight by announcing his plans to go hunting, and then leaving spikes in the window to catch the lover. The medieval nobility's passion for hunting combined with the Ovidian connotations of the love hunt and the predatory aspect of selfish passion make the hunt a particularly effective symbol in the *lais.* The hunter may play the role of the jealous, possessive husband, with the hero, in the form of an animal, but a predatory one, as the prey.

Since we lack precise or complete information about Marie's dependence on and transformation of earlier narrative material, especially Celtic, we cannot accurately judge the extent of her influence on the creators of subsequent *lais* (i.e., short narratives about love and sometimes adventure, whether or not they are called *lais* by their authors). There are, however, many *lais* and romances whose direct debts to Marie have been widely accepted.[22] Nine of the *lais* are more or less closely translated into Old Norse in a thirteenth-century manuscript now in the library of the University of Uppsala, Sweden. In Middle English, there is a truncated translation of *Le Fresne,* and three versions of *Lanval,* two from the fourteenth century and, the best known, Thomas Chestre's *Launfal Miles,* from the fifteenth. The story of *Laustic* is retold in the late twelfth-century English poem *The Owl and the Nightingale,* in Alexander of Neckham's thirteenth-century *De naturis rerum*

and in the fourteenth-century *Roman de Renart le contrefait,*
which also contains a story apparently influenced by *Bisclavret.*
We also see *Bisclavret*'s influence in the thirteenth-century *lai*
of *Melion.*

The anonymous thirteenth-century *lais* of *Tyolet, Tydorel,*
and *Guingamor,* attributed to Marie by early editors, all show
Marie's influence, with *Guingamor* owing debts to *Guigemar*
and *Lanval. Lanval* was especially popular; beside the Middle
English versions already mentioned, its influence appears
within longer poems in Middle High German and Italian.
Other long narratives inspired by Marie's *lais* include Gautier
d'Arras' *Ille et Galeron,* almost certainly based on *Eliduc,*[23]
Hue de Roteland's *Ipomedon* (c. 1185), where brothers who
are unknown to each other meet in chivalric combat and
discover their kinship thanks to a ring given to one of them
by their mother (cf. *Milun*) and Jean Renart's *Galeran
de Bretagne* (c. 1230), based on *Le Fresne.* Several elements
of the plot of *Partenopeu de Blois* (1180–1190?)—the white
deer, the pilotless ship that takes the hero to his future mistress,
their discovery after a period of secret love—recall *Guigemar,*
but both versions may have a common source, now lost.

The greatest Middle English "Breton *lai,*" *Sir Orfeo,* is,
according to its most recent editor, A. J. Bliss, a fourteenth-
century translation of a lost French original; Bliss also argues
for a common authorship of *Orfeo* and the Middle English
translation of *Le Fresne* (*Lay le Freyne*).[24] Geoffrey Chaucer
appears to have known *Sir Orfeo* and used its prologue for his
version of a Breton *lai,* the Franklin's Tale.[25] Chaucer's interest
in the problems created for a faithful wife by her husband's
departure from home in quest of chivalric honor recalls the
situation of *Milun,* but there exists no evidence to support a
suggestion that he knew, directly or in translation, Marie's *lais.*

The influence of Marie's *lais* was by no means negligible
in later medieval generations. A more recent debt to Marie
may be noted in closing: John Fowles' collection of tales, *The
Ebony Tower* (1974), is in part based on *Eliduc;* in a "personal
note," the author pays tribute to Marie, speaks about her life

and her art, and appends a translation of *Eliduc* into prose.[26]

The twelve *lais* are found in one mid-thirteenth-century manuscript (H), British Museum, Harley 978, in the order followed in this translation. Nine of the *lais*, in a different order, are preserved in a late-thirteenth-century manuscript (S), Bibliothèque nationale, nouv. acq. fr. 1104. Fragments or single *lais* appear in three other thirteenth- and fourteenth-century manuscripts: (P), Bibl. nat. fr. 2168; (C), British Museum Cott. Vesp. B XIV; (Q), Bibl. nat. fr. 24432. The Warnke edition (1900) follows (H) with additions from (S) and (P); Ewert (1947) and Rychner (1966) follow (H), and Rychner includes a few passages from (S). We have followed Ewert's text (H) in this translation, checked against Rychner.

Marie's language is quite simple, and therefore difficult to render in good literary English. There are few complex sentences and little use of the passive voice. Marie wrote in octosyllabic couplets, a form which cannot be reproduced in English without a distorting, singsong effect. We have, therefore, chosen the standard English expedient of free verse, giving the translation line by line (except for a few unavoidable transpositions) in order to catch something, however little, of the poetic quality of the original. Marie rarely names the characters in her tales and often refers to them by pronouns; where this creates confusion, we have substituted a noun or, when possible, a name. She often shifts from one scene to another with no indication other than "but" or "then"; the reader must be alert to such changes.

The translation remains close to the text, allowing for idiomatic differences between Middle French and modern English (e.g., *soz ciel* may be translated "on earth," rather than "beneath heaven"). Where Marie seems to give a word particular importance by repeating it, we repeat it in the translation. On the other hand, the stylistic device of paired synonyms, not uncommon in twelfth-century French poetry, we have respected only where it does not distort English usage. But words like *aventure,* which can mean "adventure," "chance," or "happening," are translated differently according to the context. *Chambre* is rendered as "chamber" or "room" depending on whether the reference seems to be formal or intimate. *Curteis* is usually translated as "courteous," although it carries the sense of "courtly." Where the verb tenses shift between past and present, as is common in medieval French texts, we have retained in accordance with English narrative usage a single tense throughout a passage. The titles of the *lais* are given in French with the English translation in parentheses, unless the title is a proper name.

We are especially indebted to Lawton P. G. Peckham for his generous and careful reading of the translations and his most helpful suggestions; any errors that may have crept in are the responsibility of the translators. We extend thanks as well to John Thaxton of E.P. Dutton for his interest in this translation, his suggestions for improving it, and his labors to bring it to early publication.

1. For the most reliable up-to-date information about Marie and her works, see E. J. Mickel, Jr., *Marie de France* (New York: Twayne, 1974).

2. E. Winkler identified her with Marie de Champagne, daughter of Louis VII and Eleanor, but this is not generally accepted. (For full reference, see bibliography.)

3. E. Levi argues for his son, Henri au Court Mantel, crowned in 1171, died 1183, but this identification has had little support from other scholars.

4. Strong arguments are made for William of Mandeville by Ahlström and Painter, which are accepted by Mickel, Brugger, and Rychner, e.g., that the clerks of the exchequer often referred to him simply as Count William, as Marie does in her dedication of the fables, while other nobles were named by their counties. Recently Antoinette Knapton suggested William of Warren, in a paper delivered at the Courtly Literature Society meeting, San Francisco, Dec. 27, 1975.

5. Fox, Ewert, and Wind, support the abbess of Shaftesbury; Levi opts for the abbess of Reading, Holmes and Whichard for Marie de Meulan, and Knapton for Marie de Boulogne, younger daughter of King Stephen of England, abbess of Ramsey, later married to Matieu of Flanders.

6. Both Ewert and Rychner, recent editors of the *Lais,* accept this order.

7. See Mickel, p. 17, on the later date.

8. Ewert and Illingworth date them 1155–70, Rychner, 1160–70.

9. Ewert, Illingworth and Rychner, in particular.

10. Fourrier dates *Ille* c. 1178; Mickel gives it a *terminus post quem* of 1185.

11. Béroul's poem may have been written in some form as early as 1165, but references in the extant version put it as late as 1191. If one dates Thomas

1160–65, Marie may have known his poem, as Hoepffner, Levi and Wind think; Martineau-Génieys thinks Thomas wrote after Marie and drew on her work.

12. Mickel notes that Lanval is mentioned in *Guillaume de Dole,* written c. 1200, and that Dol was no longer an archbishopric, as it is referred to in *Fresne,* after 1199, so the *lai* must have been written by then.

13. Mickel points to a number of similarities between the fables and the *lais,* in narrative methods, in the attitude towards reality, in feudal morality, p. 37.

14. See Spitzer, Mickel ("A Reconsideration"), and Damon, the latter for a psychological analysis of the *lais.*

15. See Frey.

16. For a similar phenomenon in Chrétien de Troyes, see W. T. H. Jackson, "Problems of Communication in the Romances of Chrétien de Troyes," *Medieval Literature and Folklore Studies: essays in honor of F. L. Utley,* ed. J. Mandel and B. A. Rosenberg (New Brunswick: Rutgers University Press, 1970), pp. 39–50.

17. See M. H. Ferguson, for an interesting study of Marie's use of folklore motifs and her twisting of the conventional story patterns in order to present the realistic view.

18. See H. S. Robertson, "Love and the Other World." Mickel notes that the courtly elite enclosed themselves in a world forbidden to the profane on the spiritual level, not unlike the other-world in Celtic myth, *Marie de France,* p. 64.

19. See Cotrell.

20. See Stevens.

21. See Mickel, "Marie de France's Use of Irony."

22. Much of this material on her influence is taken from Ewert's introduction and notes to his edition.

23. See P. Nykrog, "Two Creators of Narrative Form in Twelfth Century France: Gautier d'Arras—Chrétien de Troyes," *Speculum* 48 (1973), 258–76, for a discussion of Gautier's use of Marie's *lai.*

24. *Sir Orfeo,* ed. A. J. Bliss (Oxford University Press, 1954), pp. xxxif., xliv–xlvii.

25. See L. H. Loomis, "Chaucer and the Breton Lays of the Auchinleck MS," *Studies in Philology,* 38 (1941), 18–29.

26. John Fowles, *The Ebony Tower* (New York: New American Lib., repr. 1975), pp. 107–133.

Prologue

Whoever has received knowledge
and eloquence in speech from God
should not be silent or secretive
but demonstrate it willingly.
5 When a great good is widely heard of,
then, and only then, does it bloom,
and when that good is praised by many,
it has spread its blossoms.
The custom among the ancients—
10 as Priscian testifies—
was to speak quite obscurely
in the books they wrote,
so that those who were to come after
and study them
15 might gloss the letter
and supply its significance from their own wisdom.
Philosophers knew this,
they understood among themselves
that the more time they spent,
20 the more subtle their minds would become[1]
and the better they would know how to keep themselves
from whatever was to be avoided.
He who would guard himself from vice
should study and understand
25 and begin a weighty work
by which he might keep vice at a distance,
and free himself from great sorrow.
That's why I began to think
about composing some good stories
30 and translating from Latin to Romance;

1. In this reading we have followed Mickel's suggestion, to ignore the emendation of *trespassereit* and take the (H) reading *trespasserunt* ("The Unity and Significance of Marie's Prologue"). The other way, these lines would mean "the more time went by, the more difficult the sense became, and the more care they must take to find what might be overlooked."

but that was not to bring me fame:
too many others have done it.
Then I thought of the *lais* I'd heard.
I did not doubt, indeed I knew well,
35 that those who first began them[2]
and sent them forth
composed them in order to preserve
adventures they had heard.
I have heard many told;
40 and I don't want to neglect or forget them.
To put them into word[3] and rhyme
I've often stayed awake.

In your honor, noble King,
who are so brave and courteous,
45 repository of all joys
in whose heart all goodness takes root,
I undertook to assemble these *lais*
to compose and recount them in rhyme.
In my heart I thought and determined,
50 sire, that I would present them to you.
If it pleases you to receive them,
you will give me great joy;
I shall be happy forever.
Do not think me presumptuous
55 if I dare present them to you.
Now hear how they begin.

2. The order of the next four lines has been shifted; in the French ll. 37–38 precede ll. 35–36.

3. *Ditié* can be a moral saying or a song. It may refer to the *surplus*, the glossed meaning, what Robertson calls the doctrinal content, or to the fact that the *lais* were sung, cf. *Guigemar*, ll. 885–86.

Guigemar

Whoever deals with good material
feels pain if it's treated improperly.
Listen, my lords, to the words of Marie,
who does not forget her responsibilities when her turn comes.[1]

5 People should praise anyone
who wins admiring comments for herself.
But anywhere there is
a man or a woman of great worth,
people who envy their good fortune
10 often say evil things about them;
they want to ruin their reputations.
Thus they act like
vicious, cowardly dogs
who bite people treacherously.
15 I don't propose to give up because of that;
if spiteful critics or slanderers
wish to turn my accomplishments against me,
they have a right to their evil talk.
    The tales—and I know they're true—
20 from which the Bretons made their *lais*
I'll now recount for you briefly;
and at the very beginning of this enterprise,
just the way it was written down,
I'll relate an adventure
25 that took place in Brittany,
in the old days.
    At that time, Hoel ruled Brittany,
sometimes peacefully, sometimes at war.
The king had a vassal

---

1. The French *en sun tens* could also be rendered, "in her day"; Rychner
opts for this sense, seeing in it an implied contrast between Marie as a modern
writer and the ancient writers and sages referred to in the Prologue to the
whole collection.

30 who was lord of Leonnais;
his name was Oridial
and he was on very intimate terms with his lord.
A worthy and valiant knight,
he had, by his wife, two children,
35 a son and a beautiful daughter.
The girl's name was Noguent;
they called the boy Guigemar.
There wasn't a more handsome youngster in the kingdom.
His mother had a wonderful love for him,
40 and his father a great devotion;
when he could bring himself to part with the boy,
his father sent him to serve the king.
The boy was intelligent and brave,
and made himself loved by all.
45 When his time of probation was at an end,
and he was mature in body and mind,
the king dubbed him knight,
giving him luxurious armor, which was exactly what he desired.
Guigemar left the court,
50 but not before dispensing many rich gifts.
      He journeyed to Flanders to seek his fame;
there was always a war, or a battle raging there.
Neither in Lorraine nor in Burgundy,
in Anjou nor in Gascony,
55 could one find, in those days,
Guigemar's equal as a fine knight.
But in forming him nature had so badly erred
that he never gave any thought to love.
There wasn't a lady or a maid on earth,
60 no matter how noble, or how beautiful,
who wouldn't have willingly granted him her love,
had he asked her for it.
Many maids asked him,
but he wasn't interested in such things;
65 no one could discover in him
the slightest desire to love.

Therefore both friends and strangers
gave him up for lost.
    At the height of his fame,
70 this baron, Guigemar, returned to his own land
to visit his father and his lord,
his good mother and his sister,
all of whom were most eager to see him.
Guigemar stayed with them,
75 I believe, an entire month.
Then he was seized by a desire to hunt;
that night he summoned his companions in arms,
his huntsmen, and his beaters;
next morning he set out for the woods
80 to indulge in the sport that gave him much pleasure.
They gathered in pursuit of a great stag;
the dogs were unleashed.
The hunters ran ahead
while the young man lingered behind;
85 a squire carried his bow,
his hunting knife, and his quiver.[2]
He wanted to fire some arrows, if he had the opportunity,
before he left that spot.
In the thickest part of a great bush
90 Guigemar saw a hind with a fawn;
a completely white beast,
with deer's antlers on her head.
Spurred by the barking of the dogs, she sprang into the open.
Guigemar took his bow and shot at her,
95 striking her in the breastbone.[3]
She fell at once,
but the arrow rebounded,
gave Guigemar such a wound—
it went through his thigh right into the horse's flank—

---

2. As practiced by the medieval aristocracy, the hunt proceeded according
to precise, complicated rules that governed the actions of each participant.
    3. "Breastbone": so Rychner glosses *esclot;* Ewert reads, "front hoof."

100 that he had to dismount.
He collapsed on the thick grass
beside the hind he'd struck.
The hind, wounded as she was,
suffered pain and groaned.
105 Then she spoke, in this fashion:
"Alas! I'm dying!
And you, vassal, who wounded me,
this be your destiny:
may you never get medicine for your wound!
110 Neither herb nor root,
neither physician nor potion,
will cure you
of that wound in your thigh,
until a woman heals you,
115 one who will suffer, out of love for you,
pain and grief
such as no woman ever suffered before.
And out of love for her, you'll suffer as much;
the affair will be a marvel
120 to lovers, past and present,
and to all those yet to come.
Now go away, leave me in peace!"
❦ Guigemar was badly wounded;
what he had heard dismayed him.
125 He began to consider carefully
what land he might set out for
to have his wound healed.
He didn't want to remain there and die.
He knew, he reminded himself,
130 that he'd never seen a woman
to whom he wanted to offer his love,
nor one who could cure his pain.
He called his squire to him;
"Friend," he said, "go quickly!
135 Bring my companions back here;
I want to talk to them."

The squire rode off and Guigemar remained;
he complained bitterly to himself.
Making his shirt into a bandage,
140 he bound his wound tightly;
Then he mounted his horse and left that spot.
He was anxious to get far away;
he didn't want any of his men to come along,
who might interfere, or try to detain him.
145 Through the woods he followed
a grassy path, which led him
out into open country; there, at the edge of the plain,
he saw a cliff and a steep bank
overlooking a body of water below:
150 a bay that formed a harbor.
There was a solitary ship in the harbor;
Guigemar saw its sail.
It was fit and ready to go,
calked outside and in—
155 no one could discover a seam in its hull.
Every deck rail and peg
was solid ebony;
no gold under the sun could be worth more.
The sail was pure silk;
160 it would look beautiful when unfurled.
The knight was troubled;
he had never heard it said
anywhere in that region
that ships could land there.
165 He went down to the harbor
and, in great pain, boarded the ship.
He expected to discover men inside,
guarding the vessel,
but he saw no one, no one at all.
170 Amidships he found a bed
whose posts and frame

were wrought in the fashion of Solomon,[4]
of cypress and ivory,
with designs in inlaid gold.
175 The quilt on the bed was made
of silken cloth, woven with gold.
I don't know how to estimate the value of the other bedclothes,
but I'll tell you this much about the pillow:
whoever rested his head on it
180 would never have white hair.
The sable bedspread
was lined with Alexandrian silk.
Two candelabra of fine gold—
the lesser of the two worth a fortune—
185 were placed at the head of the cabin,
lighted tapers placed in them.
❧ Guigemar, astonished by all this,
reclined on the bed
and rested; his wound hurt.
190 Then he rose and tried to leave the ship,
but he couldn't return to land.
The vessel was already on the high seas,
carrying him swiftly with it.
A good, gentle wind was blowing,
195 so turning back now was out of the question.
Guigemar was very upset; he didn't know what to do.
It's no wonder he was frightened,
especially as his wound was paining him a great deal.
Still, he had to see the adventure through.
200 He prayed to God to watch over him,
to use his power to bring him back to land,
and to protect him from death.

4. Rychner notes that this term referred during the Middle Ages to a cer-
tain type of inlaid work. There is, however, also a widely diffused medieval
legend about a marvelous ship made by Solomon that intrudes into some
versions of the story of the Grail, and moreover the description of the bed
contains reminiscences of the biblical Song of Solomon (see Ewert's note).

He lay down on the bed, and fell asleep.
That day he'd survived the worst;
205 before sundown he would arrive
at the place where he'd be cured—
near an ancient city,
the capital of its realm.
The lord who ruled over that city
210 was a very aged man who had a wife,
a woman of high lineage,
noble, courteous, beautiful, intelligent;
he was extremely jealous,
which accorded with his nature.
215 (All old folk are jealous;
every one of them hates the thought of being cuckolded,
such is the perversity of age.)
The watch he kept over her was no joke.
The grove beneath the tower
220 was enclosed all around
with walls of green marble,
very high and thick.
There was only one entrance,
and it was guarded day and night.
225 On the other side, the sea enclosed it;
no one could enter, no one leave,
except by means of a boat,
as the castle might require it.
Inside the castle walls,
230 the lord had built a chamber—
none more beautiful anywhere—to keep his wife under guard—
At its entrance was a chapel.
The room was painted with images all around;
Venus the goddess of love
235 was skillfully depicted in the painting,
her nature and her traits were illustrated,
whereby men might learn how to behave in love,
and to serve love loyally.
Ovid's book, the one in which he instructs

240 lovers how to control their love,
    was being thrown by Venus into a fire,
    and she was excommunicating all those
    who ever perused this book
    or followed its teachings.[5]
245 That's where the wife was locked up.
    Her husband had given her
    a girl to serve her,
    one who was noble and well educated—
    she was his niece, the daughter of his sister.[6]
250 There was great affection between the two women.
    She stayed with her mistress when he went off,
    remaining with her until he returned.
    No one else came there, man or woman,
    nor could the wife leave the walls of the enclosure.
255 An old priest, hoary with age,
    kept the gate key;
    he'd lost his nether member
    or he wouldn't have been trusted.
    He said mass for her
260 and served her her food.
       That same day, as soon as she rose from a nap,
    the wife went into the grove;
    she had slept after dinner,
    and now she set out to amuse herself,
265 taking her maid with her.
    Looking out to sea,
    they saw the ship on the rising tide
    come sailing into the harbor.
    They could see nothing guiding it.
270 The lady started to flee—

5. The book in question is Ovid's *Remedia amoris* (Remedies for Love), a companion volume to the Roman poet's equally tongue-in-cheek *Ars amatoria*. E. J. Mickel notes the irony of this mural, presumably commissioned by the husband to encourage his wife to love him, but, as Marie describes it, predictive of the coming relationship between Guigemar and the young wife.

6. The French text is ambiguous as to whether the girl is the niece of the husband or the wife.

it's not surprising if she was afraid;
her face grew red from fear.
But the girl, who was wise
and more courageous,

275 comforted and reassured her,
and they went toward the water, fast as they could.
The damsel removed her cloak,
and boarded the beautiful ship.
She found no living thing

280 except the sleeping knight.
She saw how pale he was and thought him dead;
she stopped and looked at him.
Then she went back
quickly, and called her mistress,

285 told her what she'd found,
and lamented the dead man she'd seen.
The lady answered, "Let's go see him!
If he's dead, we'll bury him;
the priest will help us.

290 If I find that he's alive, he'll tell us all about this."
Without tarrying any longer, they returned together,
the lady first, then the girl.
When the lady entered the ship,
she stopped in front of the bed.

295 She examined the knight,
lamenting his beauty and fine body;
she was full of sorrow on his account,
and said it was a shame he'd died so young.
She put her hand on his breast,

300 and felt that it was warm, and his heart healthy,
beating beneath his ribs.
The knight, who was only asleep,
now woke up and saw her;
he was delighted, and greeted her—

305 he realized he'd come to land.
The lady, upset and weeping,
answered him politely

and asked him how
he got there, what country he came from,
310 if he'd been exiled because of war.
"My lady," he said, "not at all.
But if you'd like me to tell you
the truth, I'll do so;
I'll hide nothing from you.
315 ❦ I come from Brittany.
Today I went out hunting in the woods,
and shot a white hind;
the arrow rebounded,
giving me such a wound in the thigh
320 that I've given up hope of being cured.
The hind complained and spoke to me,
cursed me, swore
that I'd never be healed
except by a girl;
325 I don't know where she might be found.
❦ When I heard my destiny,
I quickly left the woods:
I found this boat in a harbor,
and made a big mistake: I went on board.
330 The boat raced off to sea with me on it;
I don't know where I've arrived,
or what this city's called.
Beautiful one, I beg you, for God's sake,
please advise me!
335 I don't know where to go,
and I can't even steer this ship!"
❦ She answered him, "My dear lord,
I'll be happy to advise you;
this is my husband's city,
340 and so is the region around it.
He is a rich man of high lineage,
but extremely old;
he's also terribly jealous.
On my word of honor,

345 he has locked me up in this stronghold.
There's only one entrance,
and an old priest guards the gate:
may God let him burn in hell!
I'm shut in here night and day.
350 I'd never dare
to leave except at his command,
when my lord asks for me.
Here I have my room and my chapel,
and this girl lives with me.
355 If it pleases you to stay here
until you're better able to travel,
we'll be happy to put you up,
we'll serve you willingly."
When he hears this,
360 Guigemar thanks the lady warmly,
and says he'll stay with her.
He rose from the bed;
with some difficulty they supported him,
and the lady brought him to her chamber.
365 The young man lay down
on the girl's bed,
behind a drape that was hung
across her room like a curtain.
They brought him water in a golden basin,
370 washed his thigh,
and with a fine, white silk cloth
they wiped the blood from his wound.
Then they bound it tightly.
They treated him very kindly.
375 When their evening meal came,
the girl left enough of hers
for the knight to have some;
he ate and drank quite well.
But now love struck him to the quick;
380 great strife was in his heart
because the lady had wounded him so badly

that he forgot his homeland.
His other wound no longer bothered him,
but he sighed with new anguish.
385 He begged the girl, who was assigned to take care of him,
to let him sleep.
She left him and went away,
since he had requested it,
returning to her mistress,
390 who was also feeling somewhat scorched
by the same fire Guigemar felt
igniting and consuming his heart.
❧ The knight was alone now,
preoccupied and in distress.
395 He didn't yet know what was wrong,
but this much he could tell:
if the lady didn't cure him,
he was sure to die.
"Alas!" he said, "what shall I do?
400 I'll go to her and tell her
that she should have mercy and pity
on a poor, disconsolate wretch like me.
If she refuses my plea,
shows herself so proud and scornful,
405 then I'll have to die of grief,
languishing forever in this pain."
He sighed; but a little later
formed a new resolution,
and said to himself he'd have to keep suffering;
410 you have to endure what you can't change.
He lay awake all night,
sighing and in distress.
He turned over in his mind
her words and appearance,
415 the bright eyes, the fair mouth
whose sweetness had touched his heart.[7]

---

7. Reading *doucors* with MS (P), instead of Ewert's *dolur* from (H).

Under his breath he cried for mercy;
he almost called her his beloved.
If he only knew what she was feeling—
420 how love was torturing her—
I think he would have been very happy;
that little bit of consolation
would have diminished the pain
that drained him of his color.
425 If he was suffering from love of her,
she had nothing to gloat about, either.
Next morning, before dawn,
the lady arose.
She'd been awake all night, that was her complaint.
430 It was the fault of love, pressing her hard.
The damsel, who was with her,
noticed from the appearance of her lady
that she was in love
with the knight who was staying
435 in her chamber until he was healed;
but her mistress didn't know whether or not he loved her.
The lady went off to church
and the girl went off to the knight.
She sat down by the bed;
440 he spoke to her, saying,
"My dear friend, where has my lady gone?
Why did she rise so early?"
He paused, and sighed.
The girl spoke frankly:
445 "My lord," she said, "you're in love;
take care not to hide it too well!
The love you offer
may in fact be well received.
Anyone whom my lady chooses to love
450 certainly ought to think well of her.
This love would be suitable
if both of you were constant:

you're handsome and she's beautiful."
He answered the girl,
455 "I'm so in love with her
that if I don't get relief soon
I'll be in a very bad way.
Advise me, dear friend!
What should I do about my passion?"
460 The girl very sweetly
comforted the knight,
promised to help him
in every way she could;
she was very good-hearted and well bred.
465 ❧ When the lady had heard mass
she returned; she was anything but neglectful:
she wanted to know whether the man
whom she couldn't help loving
was awake or asleep.
470 The girl called her
and brought her to the knight;
now she'll have all the time she needs
to tell him what she's feeling,
for better or for worse.
475 He greeted her and she him;
they were both very scared now.
He didn't dare ask anything from her,
for he was a foreigner
and was afraid, if he told her what he felt,
480 she'd hate him for it, send him away.
But he who hides his sickness
can hardly be brought back to health;
love is a wound in the body,
and yet nothing appears on the outside.
485 It's a sickness that lasts a long time,
because it comes from nature.
Many people treat it lightly,
like these false courtiers
who have affairs everywhere they go,

490 then boast about their conquests;
that's not love but folly,
evil and lechery.
If you can find a loyal love,
you should love and serve it faithfully,
495 be at its command.
Guigemar was deeply in love;
he must either get help quickly
or live in misery.
So love inspires bravery in him:
500 he reveals his desires to the lady.
"Lady," he said, "I'm dying because of you;
my heart is full of anguish.
If you won't cure me,
I'll have to perish sooner or later.
505 I beg you to love me—
fair one, don't deny me!"
When she had heard him out,
she gave a fitting answer.
She laughed, and said, "My love,
510 I'd be ill advised to act too quickly
in granting your prayer.
I'm not accustomed to such a request."
"My lady," he replied, "for God's sake, have mercy!
Don't be annoyed if I speak like this to you.
515 It's appropriate for an inconstant woman
to make some one plead with her a long time
to enhance her worth; that way he won't think
she's used to such sport.
But a woman of good character,
520 sensible as well as virtuous,
if she finds a man to her liking,
oughtn't to treat him too disdainfully.
Rather she should love and enjoy him;
this way, before anyone knows or hears of it,
525 they'll have done a lot that's to their advantage.

Now, dear lady, let's end this discussion."
The lady realized he was telling the truth,
and immediately granted him
her love; then he kissed her.
530 From now on, Guigemar is at ease.
They lie down together and converse,
kissing and embracing often.
I hope they also enjoy whatever else
others do on such occasions.
535 ❧❧ It appears to me that Guigemar
stayed with her a year and a half.
Their life was full of pleasure.
But Fortune, who never forgets her duty,
turns her wheel suddenly,
540 raising one person up while casting another down;
and so it happened with the lovers,
because suddenly they were discovered.
❧❧ One summer morning,
the lady was lying beside her young lover;
545 she kissed his mouth and eyes,
and said to him, "Dear, sweet love,
my heart tells me I'm going to lose you.
We're going to be found out.
If you die, I want to die, too,
550 but if you can escape,
you'll go find another love
while I stay here in misery."
"Lady," he said, "don't say such a thing!
I would never have any joy or peace
555 if I turned to another woman.
You needn't be afraid of that!"
"Beloved, I need your promise.
Give me your shirt;
I'll make a knot in the tail.
560 You have my leave to love the woman,
whoever she may be,

who will be able to undo it."
He gave her the shirt, and his promise;
she made the knot in such a way
565 that no woman could untie it
except with scissors or knife.
She gave him back the shirt,
and he took it on condition
that she should make a similar pledge to him,
570 by means of a belt
that she would wear next to her bare flesh,
tightened about her flanks.
Whoever could open the buckle
without breaking it or severing it from the belt,
575 would be the one he would urge her to love.
He kissed her, and left it at that.

That day they were discovered—
spied upon and found out
by an evil, cunning chamberlain,
580 sent by the husband.
He wanted to speak with the lady,
and couldn't get into her chamber;
he looked in a window and saw the lovers,
he went and told his lord.
585 When he heard about it,
the lord was sorrier than he'd ever been before.
He called for three of his henchmen
and straightaway went to the wife's chamber;
he had the door broken down.
590 Inside he found the knight.
He was so furious
that he gave orders to kill the stranger.
Guigemar got up,
not at all afraid.
595 He grabbed a wooden rod
on which clothes were usually hung,
and waited for his assailants.

Guigemar will make some of them suffer for this;
before they get close to him,
600 he'll have maimed them all.
❀ The lord stared at him for a long time,
and finally asked him
who he was, where he came from,
how he'd gotten in there.
605 Guigemar told him how he'd come there
and how the lady had received him;
he told him all about the adventure
of the wounded hind,
about his wound and the ship;
610 now he is entirely in the other's power.
The lord replied that he didn't believe him,
but if it really was the way he had told it
and if he could find the ship,
he'd send Guigemar back out to sea.
615 If he survived, that would be a shame;
he'd be happier if Guigemar drowned.
❀ When he had made this pledge,
they went together to the harbor,
and found the ship; they put Guigemar on it—
620 it will take him back to his own land.
The ship got under way without waiting.
The knight sighed and cried,
often lamenting his lady
and praying to almighty God
625 to grant him a quick death,
and never let him come to port
if he couldn't regain his mistress,
whom he desired more than his own life.
He persisted in his grief
630 until the ship came to the port
where he'd first found it;
he was now very near his native land.
He left the ship as quickly as he could.
❀ A boy whom Guigemar had raised

635 came by, following a knight,
     and leading a war-horse.
     Guigemar recognized him and called to him;
     the squire looked at him,
     recognized his lord, dismounted,
640 and presented the charger to him.
     Guigemar went off with him; all his friends
     rejoiced that they had found him again.
     He was highly honored in his land,
     but through it all he was sad and distracted.
645 His friends wanted him to take a wife,
     but he refused them altogether;
     he'll never have to do with a woman,
     for love or money,
     if she can't untie
650 his knotted shirt without tearing it.
     The news traveled throughout Brittany;
     all the women and girls
     came to try their luck,
     but none could untie the knot.
655 Now I want to tell you about the lady
     whom Guigemar loved so dearly.
     On the advice of one of his barons,
     her husband had her imprisoned
     in a dark marble tower.
660 There she passed bad days, worse nights.
     No one in the world could describe
     the pain, the suffering,
     the anguish and the grief,
     that she endured in that tower.
665 She remained there two years and more, I believe,
     without ever having a moment of pleasure.
     Often, she mourned for her lover:
     "Guigemar, my lord, why did I ever lay eyes on you?
     I'd rather die quickly
670 than suffer this lingering torture.

My love, if I could escape,
I'd go to where you put out to sea
and drown myself." Then she got up;
in astonishment she went to the door
675 and found it unlocked;
by good fortune, she got outside—
no one bothered her.
She came to the harbor, and found the boat.
It was tied to the rock
680 where she had intended to drown herself.
When she saw it there, she went aboard;
she could think of only one thing—
that this was where her lover had perished.
Suddenly, she couldn't stand up.
685 If she could have gotten back up on deck,
she would have thrown herself overboard,
so great was her suffering.
The boat set out, taking her with it.
It came to port in Brittany,
690 beneath a strong, well-built castle.
✻ The lord of the castle
was named Meriaduc.
He was fighting a war with a neighbor,
and had risen early that morning
695 because he wanted to dispatch his troops
to attack his enemy.
Standing at a window,
he saw the ship arrive.
He went downstairs
700 and called his chamberlain;
quickly they went to the ship,
climbed up its ladder;
inside they found the woman
who had a fairylike beauty.
705 He took her by the cloak
and brought her with him to his castle.

He was delighted with his discovery,
for she was incredibly beautiful;
whoever had put her on the boat,
710 he could tell she came from high lineage.
He felt for her a love
as great as he'd ever had for a woman.
   He had a young sister,
a beautiful maiden, in his care;
715 he commended the lady to her attention.
So she was waited on and made much of;
the damsel dressed her richly.
But she remained constantly sad and preoccupied.
The lord often came to speak with her,
720 since he wanted to love her with all his heart.
He pleaded for her love; she didn't want it,
instead she showed him her belt:
she would never love any man
except the one who could open the belt
725 without breaking it. When he heard that,
Meriaduc replied angrily,
"There's another one like you in this land,
a very worthy knight,
who avoids, in a similar manner, taking a wife
730 by means of a shirt
the right tail of which is knotted;
it can't be untied
except by using scissors or a knife.
I think you must have made that knot!"
735   When the lady heard this, she sighed,
and almost fainted.
He took her in his arms,
cut the laces of her tunic,
and tried to open the belt.
740 But he didn't succeed.
There wasn't a knight in the region
whom he didn't summon to try his luck.

❦❦ Things went on like this for quite a while,
up to the time of a tournament
745 that Meriaduc had proclaimed
against the lord he was fighting.
He sent for knights and enlisted them in his service,
knowing very well that Guigemar would come.
He asked him as a special favor,
750 as his friend and companion,
not to let him down in this hour of need,
but to come help him.
So Guigemar set out, richly supplied,
leading more than one hundred knights.
755 Meriaduc entertained him
as an honored guest in his stronghold.
He then sent two knights to his sister,
and commanded her
to prepare herself and come to him,
760 bringing with her the woman he so much loved.
The girl obeyed his order.
Lavishly outfitted,
they came hand in hand into the great hall.
The lady was pale and upset;
765 she heard Guigemar's name
and couldn't stand up.
If the damsel hadn't supported her,
she'd have fallen to the ground.
Guigemar arose when the women entered;
770 he looked at the lady and noticed
her appearance and behavior;
involuntarily, he shrank back a bit.
"Is this," he said, "my dear love,
my hope, my heart, and my life—
775 my beautiful lady who loved me?
Where did she come from? Who brought her here?
Now, that was a foolish thought!
I know it can't be she;
women often look alike—

780 I got all excited for no reason.
But because she looks like the one
for whom my heart aches and sighs,
I'll gladly speak to her."
Then the knight came forward,

785 he kissed her and sat her down beside him;
he didn't say another word,
except that he asked her to sit down.
Meriaduc looked at them closely,
upset by the sight of them together.

790 He called Guigemar cheerfully:
"My lord," he said, "please
let this girl try
to untie your shirt,
to see if she can manage to do it."

795 Guigemar answered, "Certainly."
He summoned a chamberlain
who was in charge of the shirt
and commanded him to bring it.
It was given to the girl,

800 but she couldn't untie it at all.
The lady knew the knot very well;
her heart is greatly agitated,
for she would love to try to untie it,
if she dared and could.

805 Meriaduc saw this clearly;
he was as sorry as he could be.
"My lady," he said, "now try
to untie it, if you can."
When she heard his order,

810 she took the shirttail
and easily untied the knot.
Guigemar was thunderstruck;
he knew her very well, and yet
he couldn't bring himself to believe firmly it was she.

815 So he spoke to her in this way:

"Beloved, sweet creature,
is that you? Tell me truly!
Let me see your body,
and the belt I put on you."
820 He put his hands on her hips,
and found the belt.
"My beautiful one," he said, "what a lucky adventure
that I've found you like this!
Who brought you here?"
825 She told him about the grief,
the great pains, the monotony
of the prison where she was held captive,
and everything that had happened to her—
how she escaped,
830 how she wished to drown, but found the ship instead,
and how she entered it and was brought to this port;
and how the lord of the castle kept her in custody,
guarding her in luxury
but constantly asking for her love.
835 Now her joy has returned:
"My love, take back your beloved!"
✤ Guigemar got up.
"My lords," he said, "listen to me!
Here I have the mistress
840 I thought I had lost forever.
Now I ask and implore Meriaduc
to give her back to me out of kindness.
I will become his vassal,
serve him two or three years,
845 with one hundred knights, or more!"
Meriaduc answered,
"Guigemar," he said, "my handsome friend,
I'm not so harried
or so afflicted by any war
850 that you can bargain with me about this.
I found this woman and I propose to take care of her

and defend her against you."

❦ When Guigemar heard that, he quickly
commanded his men to mount.

855 He galloped away, defying Meriaduc.[8]
It upset him to leave his beloved behind.
Guigemar took with him
every knight who had come
to the town for the tournament.

860 Each declared his loyalty to Guigemar;
they'll accompany him wherever he goes.
Whoever fails him now will truly be dishonored!
That night they came to the castle
of Meriaduc's opponent.

865 The lord of the castle put them up;
he was joyful and delighted
that Guigemar came over to his side, bringing help with him.
Now he's sure the war's as good as over.

❦ The next morning they arose,

870 and equipped themselves at their lodgings.
They departed from the village, noisily;
Guigemar came first, leading them.
Arriving at Meriaduc's castle, they assaulted it;
but it was very strong and they failed to take it.

875 Guigemar besieged the town;
he won't leave until it has fallen.
His friends and other troops increased so greatly
that he was able to starve everyone inside.
He captured and destroyed the castle,

880 killed its lord.
Guigemar led away his mistress with great rejoicing;
all his pain was now at an end.

❦ From this story that you have heard
the *lai* of Guigemar was composed,

---

8. The *defi* was a formal gesture, renouncing feudal bonds of alliance or
dependency and making it possible for one knight to attack another (or a
vassal his former lord) without incurring charges of treason.

885   which is now recited to the harp and rote;
the music is a pleasure to hear.

🌼 GUIGEMAR

IF WE JUDGE from its twenty-six-line prologue—in which Marie defends her art, and the continued practice of it, against the attacks of envious detractors—it seems that Marie intended *Guigemar* to stand at the head of her collection of *lais*. (Such an opening apologia was in fact an often-used convention of twelfth-century courtly narrative.) In *Guigemar*, Marie employs and synthesizes fairy-tale-like material (presumably of Celtic origin), contemporaneous love conventions, and situations basic to chivalric romances and *fabliaux* (short, cynical, frequently obscene tales), in order to represent metaphorically the process of growing up, and the central role desire plays in that process. The length of *Guigemar* (it is the second longest of the *lais*) allows Marie to trace the stages that bring her hero from a reflexive scorn for love, through the painful discovery of his sexuality and its powers to wound and heal, to the crisis of forming a love relationship. When the protagonist's love is tested by adversity, loyalty emerges as its crucial element, and a final twist of fortune gives the lovers a chance to seize happiness.

The story is placed in a vague Breton past, when Hoel ruled the land.[1] Guigemar, the well-beloved son of one of Hoel's vassals, finishes his apprenticeship to a king and sets out to seek honor (*pris*) as a mercenary knight.[2] His success in war contrasts sharply with his complete indifference to women and love. This rejection of the possibility of a relationship that would offer purely private fulfillment (as opposed to the public rewards of prowess: i.e., honor and fame) and the resultant deepening of self-awareness mark Guigemar as sexually and psychologically immature. In modern terms, he is engaged in the dangerous enterprise of avoiding or repressing the passionate, instinctual side of himself, which is a form of psychic self-mutilation. His refusal to be involved with women also allows Guigemar to avoid locating the source of his happiness outside himself, as would be the case if he loved, and therefore to forestall vulnerability to circumstances beyond his control, or Fortune. He chooses instead to create his own "fortune" by forcing others to submit to his strength in battle.

To dramatize the consequences and the abrupt conclusion of Guigemar's mode of living, Marie seizes upon the emblem of his penchant for hunting—a symbol, at least as old as the classical myth of Hippolytus, of aggressive self-sufficiency and repressive chastity, because in the hunt the bestial part of nature is confronted and destroyed. Guigemar encounters a white female deer with the antlers of a male, accompanied by a fawn.[3] Guigemar unleashes an arrow that wounds the hind and rebounds, severely injuring him in the thigh. This is a symbolic representation of his life to date: the hind is an image of the full sexual existence—the recognition of one's impulses toward passion as well as toward mastery (hence the creature's bisexuality)—that Guigemar has attempted to stifle and "kill" in himself, and the twin wounds suggest the deleterious effects of this policy. (Here, as in *Chaitivel,* the thigh wound is a euphemism.) Furthermore, the hind's prophecy that Guigemar will not be healed until he finds a woman, who, in curing him, will share with him a new suffering in love, would appear to represent Guigemar's concurrent awareness of the tremendous potential his newly perceived sexuality has for harm and health; it is a force that simultaneously gives and assuages misery.[4] Finally, the presumed death of the hind implies that Guigemar has ended his phase of asexual self-sufficiency. In short, the hunt of the white hind allows Marie to portray metaphorically a crisis of sexual growth and awareness in Guigemar that we associate today with adolescence.

Guigemar's realization that his wound requires treatment by an unknown woman signals his alienation from the all-male world of the hunt, with its assumption that man can seek out and control his fate, and his entry into the world of fortune with its surprises and uncertainties. Accordingly, he steals away from his companions and boards a mysterious ship, emblem of the chance (*aventure*) to which he must now consign himself in hopes of surviving. The land to which the ship brings him is the spatial embodiment of social conventions that deny and repress the love impulse from outside. A jealous old husband holds a beautiful young wife virtually captive in her chambers. Guigemar, seeking his own relief, enters this world and revives the wife by fulfilling the need for love she cannot satisfy in her loveless marriage.

If the situation of the imprisoned wife recalls the plot of many a *fabliau,* the clearly marked stages by which she and Guigemar recognize and consummate their mutual love show Marie following literary conventions developed in chivalric romances and Ovidian love tales of her day. With a characteristic blend of sentimental involvement and witty detachment, she records Guigemar's sleepless night and gradual realization of its cause; his agonized wavering between resolve to tell the lady of his desire and resignation to suffer all in silence; the exquisite moment in which the two terrified lovers make their confessions; and the brief debate (recalling the analogous but longer love dialogues of Andreas Capellanus' pseudo-textbook *De arte honeste amandi*) during which he convinces her, using delightfully spurious reasoning, that if she intends to be a loyal lover, she should grant him her favors at once—only inconstant women hesitate, to hide their lasciviousness!

The discovery of the lovers after eighteen months of secret pleasure is preceded by Marie's reference to Fortune's ever-turning wheel and by the lady's own premonition that they are about to be separated. Her fear prompts their exchange of vows of eternal loyalty, sealed and symbolized by the knot that can only be untied by the lover who made it. The change of Fortune's symbol from the ship to the wheel suggests that the lovers can no longer count on fortune for progress and continuity in their relationship, but must now transcend its hostility by drawing on the resources of the love itself. Similarly, the lady's realization that the love can no longer be kept secret reflects Marie's contention that love cannot forever remain static, secure, and untested within a womblike private world. Instead, it must grow by testing itself in the world of chance and hostile values. If love is to survive in such a world, a new virtue, loyalty, must complement and preserve passion. When the furious husband breaks in on the lovers, Guigemar reacts courageously and thus saves his life; the husband puts him back in the marvelous boat and adventure takes the grieving knight back to his own land, where his friends make much of him, but where he lives in sorrow, as unwilling as before to marry, though for a completely different reason. (The device of using repeated external situations to set off the evolving inner state of the protagonist occurs frequently in romance.)

Guigemar's insistence on marrying only the woman who will untie the knot in his shirt makes him famous and sets up the climax of the *lai*, in which he is reunited with his beloved at the castle of Meriaduc, when each unties the other's knot. Meriaduc, having taken the lady into custody after she escaped from the tower her husband had imprisoned her in and sailed away in the mysterious boat, has summoned Guigemar specifically to see if he can undo the knotted belt around the lady's body, and she his. Despite this overwhelming proof that the lovers belong only to each other, Meriaduc refuses to surrender the lady. Guigemar wins her once and for all by an act of prowess (he besieges Meriaduc's castle) that recalls his warrior life at the beginning of the *lai*, but Marie recalls his warrior consciousness only to emphasize the difference between his earlier and his later self: the knight who scorned love has become the knight who fights under its banner; his impulse to dominate is now wholly subservient to his desire to possess a woman without whom he remains incomplete.

Marie's mastery of romance conventions and her convincing, metaphoric anatomy of the stages by which love comes to dominate a life make *Guigemar* one of the most satisfying of all medieval short narratives.

1. Marie borrowed Hoel from Wace's *Roman de Brut,* a contemporary French adaptation of Geoffrey of Monmouth's fanciful *Historia regum Britanniae* (*History of the Kings of Britain*).

2. On the existence of a large floating population of young soldiers of fortune in Marie's day, see G. Duby, "Au XIIe siècle: les 'jeunes' dans la société aristocratique," *Annales* 19 (1964), 835–846.

3. Cf. Chrétien de Troyes' *Erec* and the anonymous *Partonopeu de Blois* for other twelfth-century uses of marvelous animals to activate a chivalric narrative.

4. The image of Love's medicine-tipped arrow that wounds and heals simultaneously is a commonplace of medieval love literature. Cf. Marie's comment on love's wound, 1. 483 f.

Equitan

Most noble barons
were those Bretons of Brittany.
In the old days they were accustomed, out of bravery,
courtliness, and nobility,
5 to create *lais* from the adventures they heard,
adventures that had befallen all sorts of people;
they did this as a memorial,
so that men should not forget them.
They made one that I heard—
10 it should never be forgotten—
about Equitan, a most courtly man,
the lord of Nauns, a magistrate and king.[1]

Equitan was a man of great worth,
dearly loved in his own land.
15 He loved sport and lovemaking;
and so he kept a body of knights in his service.
Whoever indulges in love without sense or moderation
recklessly endangers his life;
such is the nature of love
20 that no one involved with it can keep his head.[2]
Equitan had a seneschal,
a good knight, brave and loyal,
who took care of his land for him,
governed and administered it.
25 Unless the king was making war,
he would never, no matter what the emergency,
neglect his hunting,

---

1. The meaning and location of Nauns are subjects of scholarly dispute. Conjectures range from Nantes, in Brittany, to the kingdom of the dwarfs (*nains*). Equitan's name may, as Mickel suggests, contain a play on the Latin word for horse (*equus*), appropriate for a huntsman. Cf. further the endnote to *Milun* (note 3).

2. There is a play in the text on two meanings of *mesure*, rendered "moderation" in l. 17 and "nature" in l. 19.

his hawking, or his other amusements.

❧ This seneschal took a wife
30 through whom great harm later came to the land.
   She was a beautiful woman
   of fine breeding,
   with an attractive form and figure.
   Nature took pains in putting her together:
35 bright eyes in a lovely face,
   a pretty mouth and a well-shaped nose.
   She hadn't an equal in the entire kingdom.
   The king often heard her praised.
   He frequently sent his greetings to her,
40 presents as well;
   without having seen her, he wanted her,
   so he spoke to her as soon as he could.

❧ For his private amusement
   he went hunting in the countryside
45 where the seneschal dwelt;
   in the castle, where the lady also lived,
   the king took lodging for the night
   after he had finished the day's sport.
   He now had a good chance to speak to the wife,
50 to reveal to her his worth, his desires.
   He found her refined and clever,
   with a beautiful body and face,
   and a pleasing, cheerful demeanor.
   Love drafted him into his service:
55 he shot an arrow at the king
   that opened a great wound in the heart,
   where Love had aimed and fixed it.
   Neither good sense nor understanding were of use to the king
        now;
   love for the woman so overcame him
60 that he became sad and depressed.
   Now he has to give in to love completely;
   he can't defend himself at all.

That night he can't sleep or even rest,
instead he blames and scolds himself:
65 "Alas," he says, "what destiny
led me to these parts?
Because I have seen this woman
pain has struck at my heart,
my whole body shivers.
70 I think I have no choice but to love her—
yet if I love her, I'm doing wrong;
she's the wife of my seneschal.
I owe him the same faith and love
that I want him to give me.
75 If, by some means, he found out about this
I know how much it would upset him.
Still, it would be a lot worse
if I went mad out of concern for him.
It would be a shame for such a beautiful woman
80 not to have a lover!
What would become of her finer qualities
if she didn't nourish them by a secret love?[3]
There isn't a man in the world
who wouldn't be vastly improved if she loved him.
85 And if the seneschal should hear of the affair,
he oughtn't be too crushed by it;
he certainly can't hold her all by himself,
and I'm happy to share the burden with him!"
When he had said all that, he sighed,
90 and lay in bed thinking.
After a while, he spoke again: "Why
am I so distressed and frightened?
I still don't even know
if she will take me as her lover;
95 but I'll know soon!
If she should feel the way I do,

3. The French text refers to *druerie*, extramarital passion that would, of
course, be kept secret from the husband.

I'd soon be free of this agony.
God! It's still so long till morning!
I can't get any rest,
100 it's been forever since I went to bed."
🌿 The king stayed awake until daybreak;
he could hardly wait for it.
He rose and went hunting,
but he soon turned back
105 saying that he was worn out.
He returns to his room and lies down.
The seneschal is saddened by this;
he doesn't know what's bothering the king,
what's making him shiver;
110 in fact, his wife is the reason for it.
The king, to get some relief and some pleasure,
sends for the wife to come speak with him.
He revealed his desire to her,
letting her know that he was dying because of her;
115 that it lay in her power to comfort him
or to let him die.
"My lord," the woman said to him,
"I must have some time to think;
this is so new to me,
120 I have no idea what to say.
You're a king of high nobility,
and I'm not at all of such fortune
that you should single me out
to have a love affair with.
125 If you get what you want from me,
I have no doubt about it:
you'll soon get tired of me,
and I'll be far worse off than before.
If I should love you
130 and satisfy your desire,
love wouldn't be shared equally
between the two of us.
Because you're a powerful king

and my husband is your vassal,
135 I'm sure you believe
your rank entitles you to my love.
Love is worthless if it's not mutual.
A poor but loyal man is worth more—
if he also possesses good sense and virtue—
140 and his love brings greater joy
than the love of a prince or a king
who has no loyalty in him.
Anyone who aims higher in love
than his own wealth entitles him to
145 will be frightened by every little thing that occurs.
The rich man, however, is confident
that no one will steal a mistress away
whose favor he obtains by his authority over her."
Equitan answered her,
150 "Please, my lady! Don't say such things!
No one could consider himself noble
(rather, he'd be haggling like a tradesman)
who, for the sake of wealth or a big fief,
would take pains to win someone of low repute.
155 There's no woman in the world—if she's smart,
refined, and of noble character,
and if she places a high enough value on her love
that she isn't inconstant—
whom a rich prince in his palace
160 wouldn't yearn for
and love well and truly,
even if she'd nothing but the shirt on her back.
Whoever is inconstant in love
and gives himself up to treachery
165 is mocked and deceived in the end;
I've seen it happen many times like that.
It's no surprise when someone loses out
who deserves to because of his behavior.
My dear lady, I'm offering myself to you!
170 Don't think of me as your king,

but as your vassal and your lover.
I tell you, I promise you
I'll do whatever you want.
Don't let me die on your account!
175 You be the lord and I'll be the servant[4]—
you be the proud one and I'll be the beggar!"
❦ The king pleaded with her,
begged her so often for mercy,
that she promised him her love
180 and granted him possession of her body.
Then they exchanged rings,
and promised themselves to each other.
They kept their promises and loved each other well;
they died for this in the end.
185 ❦ Their affair lasted a long time,
without anyone hearing of it.
At the times set for their meetings,
when they were to speak together at the king's palace,
the king informed his followers
190 that he wanted to be bled privately.
The doors of his chamber were closed,
and no one was so daring,
if the king didn't summon him,
that he would ever enter there.
195 Meanwhile, the seneschal held court
and heard pleas and complaints.
The king loved the seneschal's wife for a long time,
had no desire for any other woman;
he didn't want to marry,
200 and never allowed the subject to be raised.
His people held this against him,
and the seneschal's wife
heard about it often; this worried her,
and she was afraid she would lose him.
205 So when she next had the chance to speak to him—

---

4. The French text has *dame* and *servant*.

when she should have been full of joy,
kissing and embracing him
and having a good time with him—
she burst into tears, making a big scene.
210 The king asked
what the matter was,
and the lady answered,
"My lord, I'm crying because of our love,
which has brought me to great sorrow:
215 you're going to take a wife, some king's daughter,
and you will get rid of me;
I've heard all about it, I know it's true.
And—alas!—what will become of me?
On your account I must now face death,
220 for I have no other comfort than you."
The king spoke lovingly to her:
"Dear love, don't be afraid!
I promise I'll never take a wife,
never leave you for another.
225 Believe me, this is the truth:
If your husband were dead,
I'd make you my lady and my queen;
no one could stop me."
The lady thanked him,
230 said she was very grateful to him;
if he would assure her
that he wouldn't leave her for someone else,
she would quickly undertake
to do away with her lord.
235 It would be easy to arrange
if he were willing to help her.
He agreed to do so;
there was nothing she could demand of him
that he wouldn't do, if he possibly could,
240 whether it turned out well or badly.
    "My lord," she says, "please
come hunting in the forest,

out in the country where I live.
Stay awhile at my husband's castle;
245 you can be bled there,
and on the third day after that, take a bath.[5]
My lord will be bled with you
and will bathe with you as well;
make it clear to him—and don't relent—
250 that he must keep you company!
I'll have the baths heated
and the two tubs brought in;
his will be so boiling hot
that no man on earth
255 could escape being horribly scalded
as soon as he sat down in it.
When he's scalded to death,
send for his men and yours;
then you can show them exactly how
260 he suddenly died in his bath."
The king promised her
that he'd do just as she wished.
❧ Less than three months later,
the king went out into the countryside to hunt.
265 He had himself bled to ward off illness,
and his seneschal bled with him.
On the third day, he said he wanted to bathe;
the seneschal was happy to comply.
"Bathe with me," said the king,
270 and the seneschal replied, "Willingly."
The wife had the baths heated,
the two tubs brought;
next to the bed, according to plan,
she had them both set down.
275 Then she had boiling water brought
for the seneschal's tub.

5. Baths were taken much less frequently in the Middle Ages than now
and would normally be planned in advance.

The good man got up
and went outside to relax for a moment.
His wife came to speak to the king
280 and he pulled her down beside him;
they lay down on her husband's bed
and began to enjoy themselves.
They lay there together.
Because the tub was right before them,
285 they set a guard at the bedroom door;
a maidservant was to keep watch there.
Suddenly the seneschal returned,
and knocked on the door; the girl held it closed.
He struck it so violently
290 that he forced it open.
There he discovered the king and his own wife
lying in each other's arms.
The king looked up and saw him coming;
to hide his villainy
295 he jumped into the tub feet first,
stark naked.
He didn't stop to think what he was doing.
And there he was scalded to death,
caught in his own evil trap,
300 while the seneschal remained safe and sound.
The seneschal could see very well
what had happened to the king.
He grabbed his wife at once
and thrust her head first into the tub.
305 Thus both died,
the king first, the wife after him.
Whoever wants to hear some sound advice
can profit from this example:
he who plans evil for another
310 may have that evil rebound back on him.
It all happened just as I've told you.
The Bretons made a *lai* about it,

about Equitan, his fate,
and the woman who loved him so much.

❦ EQUITAN

EQUITAN has been criticized by some scholars for its unsym-
pathetic protagonists and for the doggedly didactic tone in
which it tells the story of their illicit love and its punishment.
That the *lai* is admonitory cannot be denied. The *fabliau*-like
story of a king who betrays his own seneschal by loving the
latter's wife, and then plots with her the seneschal's death only
to have the plan backfire fatally, allows Marie to draw an
unequivocal concluding moral: he who plans evil for another
may find the evil falling upon himself. At the beginning of
the tale, she had already signaled its exemplary nature by
another sententious statement about love: those who love ir-
rationally, and excessively, court danger, for love prevents the
lover from acting reasonably in the best of circumstances.
Connecting the two framing *sententiae,* the intervening nar-
rative illustrates with pitiless clarity the inevitable progress
from the king's passion—which he cannot or will not control,
though he knows it violates the loyalty he owes a devoted
vassal—to his involvement in the murder plot. When, just
before the murder is to take place, the king once again gives
in to his passion, and makes love with the seneschal's wife
on her husband's bed, he seals his own fate: the seneschal
bursts into the chamber, and the king, in total confusion,
leaps into the bathtub of scalding water intended for the
victim. Equitan, that is, becomes the victim of his own plot,
as he has been the victim of his own irresistible desire. The
tub of boiling water thus becomes a double emblem: of the
trickster tricked, and of the immoderate lover fatally burned
by his ungoverned passion.

Marie's artistic intent functions at two levels besides the didactic-exemplary in *Equitan*. First, the *lai* functions as a negative version of some of the twelfth-century love conventions sympathetically represented in *Guigemar*. The situations of the two protagonists are similar: both are hunters; both experience the first sufferings of love during a sleepless night and soliloquize about their pains and fears; the commonplace of love as a wound is applied to both; both woo married women and overcome their objections in dialogues of a casuistical type that were popular in the twelfth century. Finally, after a long, happy period of secret liaisons, each pair of lovers is discovered by the husband.

Within this network of parallels, Marie subverts or inverts in *Equitan* the attitudes of *Guigemar*. In the king's love monologue, he blames destiny for leading him to the wife's land (cf. Guigemar's ship), whereas he had deliberately come to the seneschal's castle, ostensibly on a hunting trip, but actually to meet the woman of whose beauty he had heard so much. (The hunt, in *Equitan*, leads not to a symbolic encounter, as it does in *Guigemar*, but to a real one; the king's "hunt" for sexual gratification reminds us that there was a substantial medieval literature in which love was represented allegorically as a hunt.)[1] The theme of loyalty in love, emblematically represented by the knots tied by the protagonists in *Guigemar*, receives dubious scrutiny in *Equitan*: the king recognizes at once that he will do wrong in loving the wife of a man to whom he owes the same faith he expects from him, but he beats back this knowledge with cynical arguments that his own sanity and the lady's *courtoisie* both require the love affair for their continuity. He even tells himself, with mock earnestness, that he is only going to help the seneschal bear the burden of his beautiful wife—an obvious double entendre.

Later, when the wife parries Equitan's declaration of love by saying that she would rather love a poor but loyal man than a powerful one who feels his rank entitles him to abandon her whenever he wishes, the king insists that only *her* loyalty matters to him, not any difference in their fortunes. In fact, in receiving him as her lover, she is joining Equitan in a monumental act of disloyalty to her husband. Later, in the face of his barons' plea that he marry, the wife forces Equitan to prove his fidelity to her by agreeing to help her kill the seneschal so he can marry her. Thus love-loyalty and vicious disloyalty to the marriage bond are inextricably linked. As a final, negative counterpoint to *Guigemar,* Marie depicts Equitan, when he is discovered by the seneschal, not as one emboldened by desperate love, but as a panic-stricken criminal who rushes in confusion to his own doom.

A further level of meaning in *Equitan* comprises an examination of the king's surrender of various facets of his public and private identities in his dealings with the other characters. Equitan is introduced as king and *jostise,* or administrator of justice to his people. Yet at once we are told that the king refused to leave his life of hunting and pleasure for any reason but war, and that, in his absence, the loyal seneschal protected the land and *justisoit,* administered justice. In other words, the seneschal had assumed a good part of the burdens of kingship, a fact that makes Equitan's offer to assume part of the burden of his wife an ironic completion of an exchange of roles. (The seneschal's assumption of the king's identity as judge reveals an excess, as it were, of loyalty, while the king's assumption of the seneschal's role of husband reveals a deficiency of loyalty.)

Later, in response to the lady's doubts about becoming the mistress of a king who could tyrannize over her, Equitan urges her to think of herself as a proud lady, and him a vassal, servant, and petitioner. To assuage his passion, Equitan surrenders his status to the wife, as he has previously surrendered his judicial role to the husband. Once the love affair has begun in earnest, the king enjoys his mistress behind closed doors, while outside the seneschal holds court and hears claims— again fulfilling the *judicial* function the king has abdicated to him, while Equitan assumes the role of husband the seneschal has (unknowingly) abdicated to him!

This exchange of identities—the king's public for the seneschal's private—continues until the king and the wife make love on the seneschal's own bed; Equitan has at this point gone further than ever before toward assuming the seneschal's identity. But in doing so, he exposes himself to maximum danger. The seneschal barges back into the chamber—not, presumably, because he suspects anything, but because he has been commanded by the king to be with him in private. The king, discovered in his adultery, completes his assimilation of the seneschal's identity with a final leap into the other's tub, thus appropriating the seneschal's death as well. Meanwhile, the seneschal kills the wife—an act of retribution that finalizes his assumption of the king's public identity as meter-out of justice. (Of course, at his death, the king also for the first time earns his title of *jostise* by condemning himself to death; but, as opposed to the seneschal's deliberate act of judgment, his is accidental.) The deepest irony of *Equitan* is therefore that the king's escape from the responsibilities of his public identity, already clear when the *lai* begins, is paralleled, as the *lai* unfolds, by a similar escape into the private identity of the seneschal, and that, when the process is complete, the king has destroyed himself physically as well as metaphysically.

The tight and multileveled construction of *Equitan* would seem to belie, at least in part, the contention by some critics that it is an early and inferior work of Marie. In its own fashion, it is a highly accomplished poem.

1. Mickel, in his essay on irony (see bibliography), explores the implications of the hunting metaphor for this *lai*.

Le Fresne *(The Ash Tree)*

I shall tell you the *lai* of Le Fresne
according to the story as I know it.
In olden days there lived in Brittany
two knights who were neighbors;
5 both were rich men,
brave and worthy knights.
They lived close by, within the same region;
each was married.
Now one of the wives became pregnant;
10 when her time came
she gave birth to twins.
Her husband was absolutely delighted;
in his joy at the event
he sent word to his good neighbor
15 that his wife had had two sons—
he had that many more children now.
He would send one to him to raise,
and name the child after him.
The rich neighbor was sitting down to eat
20 when the messenger arrived;
he knelt before the high table
to announce his news.
The lord thanked God for it
and rewarded him with a fine horse.
25 The knight's wife laughed
(she was seated next to him at dinner)
because she was deceitful and proud,
evil-tongued and envious.
She spoke very foolishly,
30 saying, for all her household to hear,
"So help me God, I can't imagine
where this worthy man got such advice
to announce to my lord,
to his own shame and dishonor,

73

35 that his wife has had twin sons.
   Both he and she are disgraced by this;
   we know the truth of the matter all too well:
   it never was and never will be
   possible for such a thing to happen[1]—
40 that a woman could have
   two sons in one birth—
   unless two men had lain with her."
   Her lord stared fiercely at her,
   reproached her bitterly for what she said.
45 "Wife," he said, "stop that!
   You mustn't talk that way!
   The fact is that she's a woman
   who's always had a good reputation."
   But the people in the household
50 repeated the wife's words;
   the matter was widely spoken of
   and became known throughout Brittany.
   The slanderous wife was hated for it,
   and later made to suffer for it.
55 Every woman who heard about it,
   rich or poor, hated her.
   The messenger who had brought the news
   went home and told his lord everything.
   When he heard the messenger's report,
60 he became so sad he didn't know what to do.
   He hated his worthy wife because of it,
   strongly suspected her,
   and kept her under strict guard,
   even though she didn't deserve it.
65 The wife who had spoken so evilly
   became pregnant herself that same year,
   and was carrying twins—

1. Marie uses the word *aventure* here and throughout the *lai* to refer to unexpected circumstances of the kind that test the endurance and moral worth of human beings, and bring them to happiness if they deserve it.

now her neighbor has her vengeance.
She carried them until her time came;
70 then she gave birth to two daughters; she was extremely upset,
and terribly sad about the situation.
She lamented bitterly to herself:
"Alas!" she said, "what shall I do?
I'll never get any honor out of this!
75 I'm in disgrace, that's certain.
My lord and all his kin
will never believe me
when they hear about this bad luck;[2]
indeed, I condemned myself
80 when I slandered all womankind.
Didn't I say it never happened—
at least, we've never seen it happen—
that a woman could have twins
unless she had lain with two men?
85 Now that I have twins, it seems to me
my words have come back to haunt me.
Whoever slanders another
never knows when it will rebound on him;
he may speak badly about someone
90 who's more deserving of praise than he.
Now, to keep from being disgraced,
I'll have to kill one of my children!
I'd rather make that up to God
than live in shame and dishonor."
95 Those of her household who were in the bedchamber with her
comforted her and said
they wouldn't allow her to do it;
killing somebody was no joke.
    ✣✢ The lady had an attendant
100 who was of noble birth;
the lady had raised and taken care of her
and was very attached to her.

---

2. The French text has *aventure*.

This girl heard her mistress crying,
bemoaning her situation;
105 it bothered her terribly.
She came and comforted her:
"My lady," she said, "it's not worth carrying on so.
Stop grieving—that's the thing to do.
Give me one of the babies;
110 I'll take care of her for you,
so that you won't be disgraced;
you'll never see the child again.
I'll abandon her at a convent,
to which I'll carry her safe and sound.
115 Some good person will find her,
and, God willing, he'll raise her."
The lady heard what she said;
she was delighted with the idea, and promised her
that if she did her this service
120 she'd be well rewarded for it.
     They wrapped the noble child
in a linen garment,
and then in an embroidered silk robe,
which the lady's husband had brought back to her
125 from Constantinople, where he had been.
They had never seen anything so fine.
With a piece of ribbon
she tied a large ring onto the child's arm;
it contained a full ounce of pure gold,
130 and had a ruby set in it,
with lettering around the rim of the setting.
Wherever the little girl might be found,
everyone would know beyond doubt
that she came from a noble family.
135   The damsel took the baby
and left the chamber with her.
That night, after dark,
she left the town
and took the highroad

140   that led into the forest.
        She went right through the woods
        with the baby, and out the other side,
        without ever leaving the road.
        Then, far off to the right, she heard
145   dogs barking and cocks crowing;
        she knew she would be able to find a town over there.
        Quickly, she went in the direction
        of the barking.
        Soon she came
150   to a fine, prosperous town.
        There was an abbey there,
        a thriving, well-endowed one;
        I believe it held a community of nuns
        supervised by an abbess.
155   The damsel saw
        the towers, walls, and steeple of the abbey,
        and she hastened toward it,
        stopping at the front gate.
        She put down the child she was carrying
160   and knelt humbly
        to say a prayer.
        "O God," she prayed, "by your holy name,
        if it is your will,
        protect this infant from death."
165   When she'd finished praying,
        she looked behind her,
        saw a broad-limbed ash tree,
        its branches thick with leaves;
        its trunk divided into four boughs.
170   It had been planted as a shade tree.
        The girl took the baby in her arms
        and ran over to the ash tree,
        placed the child up in its branches and left her there,
        commending her to the true God.
175   Then the girl returned to her mistress
        and told her what she'd done.

    There was a porter in the abbey,
whose job it was to open the abbey gate,
to let in the people who had come
180 to hear the early service.
That morning he rose as early as usual,
lit the candles and the lamps,
rang the bells and opened the gate.
He noticed the clothes up in the ash tree,
185 and thought that someone must have stolen them,
and then left them there.
He didn't notice anything else.
As quickly as he could, he went over to the tree,
touched the clothes, and found the child there.
190 He gave thanks to God;
he did not leave the child, but took her with him
to his own dwelling.
He had a daughter who was a widow;
her husband was dead and she had a child,
195 still in the cradle, whom she was nursing.
The good man called her:
"Daughter," he said, "get up!
Light the candle, start the fire!
I've brought home a baby
200 that I found out there in the ash tree.
Nurse her for me,
then get her warm and bathe her."
The daughter obeyed him;
she lit the fire and took the baby,
205 made her warm and gave her a good bath,
then nursed her.
On the child's arm they discovered the ring,
and they saw her costly, beautiful clothes.
From these they were certain
210 that she was born of noble lineage.
    The next day, after the service,
when the abbess came out of the chapel,

the porter went to speak to her;
he wanted to tell her how, by chance,
215　he had found the child.
The abbess ordered him
to bring the child to her
just as she was found.
The porter went home,
220　willingly brought the child back,
and showed her to the abbess.
She examined the baby closely
and said she would raise her,
would treat her as her niece.
225　She strictly forbade the porter
to tell the truth about the child's discovery.
She raised the child herself,
and because she had been found in the ash tree
the abbess decided to name her "Fresne" [Ash].
230　And so people called her.
❀ The abbess did indeed treat her as a niece,
and for a long time she grew up in privacy;
she was raised
entirely within the walls of the abbey.
235　When she reached the age
where nature creates beauty,
in all of Brittany there wasn't such a beautiful
or so refined a girl;
she was noble and cultivated
240　in appearance and speech.
Everyone who saw her loved her,
praised her to the skies.
Now at Dole there lived a good lord—
there's never been a better, before or since—
245　whose name I'll tell you here:
they called him Gurun in that region.
He heard about the young girl
and he fell in love with her.
He went to a tournament,

250   and on his way back passed the abbey,
      where he stopped to ask after the damsel.
      The abbess introduced her to him.
      He saw that she was beautiful and cultivated,
      wise, refined, and well educated.
255   If he couldn't win her love
      he'd consider himself very badly off indeed.
      But he was at a loss about how to proceed;
      if he came there often,
      the abbess would notice what was going on,
260   and he'd never lay eyes on the damsel again.
      He hit upon a scheme:
      he would become a benefactor of the abbey,
      give it so much of his land
      that it would be enriched forever;
265   he'd thus establish a patron's right to live there,
      so that he could come and stay whenever he chose.
      To be a member of that community
      he gave generously of his goods—
      but he had a motive
270   other than receiving pardon for his sins.
      He came there often
      and spoke to the girl;
      he pleaded so well, promised so much
      that she granted him what he desired.
275   When he was sure of her love,
      he spoke seriously with her one day.
      "Beautiful one," he said, "now that
      you've made me your lover,
      come away from here and live with me.
280   I'm sure you know
      that if your aunt found out about us
      she'd be upset,
      especially if you became pregnant right under her roof.
      In fact, she'd be furious.
285   If you'll take my advice,
      you'll come away with me.

I'll never let you down—
and I'll take good care of you."
Since she loved him deeply,
290 she willingly granted what he desired.
She went away with him;
he took her to his castle.
She brought her silk swaddling cloth and her ring with her;
that could turn out to be very fortunate for her.
295 The abbess had given them to her
and told her the circumstances
in which she had been sent to her:
she was nestled up in the ash tree,
and whoever had abandoned her there
300 had bestowed on her the garments and the ring.
The abbess had received no other possessions with her;
she had raised her as her niece.
The girl kept the tokens,[3]
locked them in a chest.
305 She took the chest away with her;
she'd no intention of leaving it behind.
    ❧ The knight who took her away
loved and cherished her greatly,
and so did all his men and servants.
310 There wasn't one, big or little,
who didn't love her for her noble character,
and honor her as well.
    ❧ She lived with him for a long time,
until the knight's vassals
315 reproached him for it.
They often urged him
to marry a noble woman,
and to get rid of this mistress of his.
They'd be pleased if he had an heir
320 who could succeed to
his land and inheritance;

---

3. The translation follows Rychner's emendation of *l'esgardat* to *les gardat*.

it would be much to their disadvantage
if he was deterred by his concubine
from having a child born in wedlock.
325 They would no longer consider him their lord
or willingly serve him
if he didn't do what they wanted.
The knight agreed
to take a wife according to their wishes,
330 so they began to look about for one.
"My lord," they said, "quite near by
lives a worthy man of your rank;
he has a daughter who is his heiress.
You'll get much land if you take her.
335 The girl's name is Codre [Hazel];
there isn't one so pretty in this region.
In exchange for the ash, when you get rid of her,
you'll have the hazel.
The hazel tree bears nuts and thus gives pleasure;
340 the ash bears no fruit.
Let us make the arrangements for the daughter;
God willing, we will get her for you."
They arranged the marriage,
obtained everyone's promise.
345 Alas! what a misfortune
that these good men didn't know
the real story about these girls[4]—
they were twin sisters!
Fresne was hidden away,
350 and her lover was to marry the other.
When she found out that he had done this,
she didn't sulk about it;
she continued to serve her lord well
and honored all his vassals.
355 The knights of the household,
the squires and serving boys

4. Again, the text has *aventure*.

were all very sad on her account;
sad because they were going to lose her.
❧ On the day of the betrothal,
360 her lord sent for his friends.
The archbishop of Dole,
another of his vassals, was there as well.
They all brought his fiancée to him.
Her mother came with her;
365 she worried about this other girl
whom the lord loved so much,
because she might try to cause trouble, if she could,
between Codre and her husband.
The mother wants her expelled from the house;
370 she'll tell her son-in-law
that he should marry her off to some good man;
that way he'll be rid of her, she thinks.
❧ They held the betrothals in grand style;
there was much celebrating.
375 Fresne was in the private chambers.
No matter what she saw,
it didn't seem to bother her;
she didn't even seem a bit angry.
She waited on the bride-to-be
380 courteously and efficiently.
Everybody who saw this
thought it a great marvel.
Her mother inspected her carefully,
and began to love and admire her.
385 She said to herself that if she'd known
what kind of a person Fresne was,
she wouldn't have let her suffer on account of her daughter Codre,
wouldn't have taken Fresne's lord away from her.
❧ That night, Fresne went
390 to make up the bed
in which the new bride was to sleep;
she took off her cloak,

and called the chamberlains to her.
She instructed them concerning the manner
395 in which the lord liked things done,
for she had seen it many times.
When they had prepared the bed,
they threw a coverlet over it.
The cloth was some old dress material;
400 the girl looked at it,
it seemed to her poor stuff;
that bothered her.
She opened a chest, took out her birth garment,
and put it on her lord's bed.
405 She did it to honor him;
the archbishop would be coming there
to bless the newlyweds in bed.
That was part of his duty.
When the chamber was empty,
410 the mother led her daughter in.
She wished to prepare her for bed,
and told her to get undressed.
She looked at the cloth on the bed;
she'd never seen such a fine one
415 except the one she'd given
to her infant daughter when she abandoned her.
Then she suddenly remembered the castaway;
her heart skipped a beat.
She called the chamberlain:
420 "Tell me," she said, "on your honor,
where was this fine silk cloth found?"
"My lady," he replied, "I'll tell you:
the girl brought it,
and threw it over the coverlet
425 because the coverlet didn't seem good enough to her.
I think the silk cloth is hers."
The mother now called Fresne,
and Fresne came to her;
she removed her cloak,

430 and the lady began questioning her:
    "My dear, don't hide anything from me!
    Where did you find this beautiful cloth?
    How did you come by it? Who gave it to you?
    Tell me at once where it came from!"
435 The girl answered her,
    "My lady, my aunt, who raised me—
    she is an abbess—gave it to me
    and ordered me to take good care of it;
    whoever sent me to be raised by her
440 had given me this, and also a ring."
    "Fair one, may I see the ring?"
    "Yes, my lady, I'll be happy to show you."
    Then Fresne brought her the ring;
    she examined it carefully.
445 She recognized it very well,
    and the silk cloth too.
    No doubt about it, now she knew—
    this was her own daughter.
    She didn't hide it, but cried out for all to hear,
450 "My dear, you are my daughter!"
    Out of pity for Fresne
    she fell over in a faint.
    When she regained consciousness,
    she quickly sent for her husband,
455 and he came, all in a fright.
    When he entered the bedroom,
    his wife threw herself at his feet,
    hugged and kissed him,
    asked his forgiveness for her crime.
460 He didn't know what this was all about;[5]
    "Wife," he said, "what are you talking about?
    There's been nothing but good between us.
    I'll pardon you as much as you please!
    Tell me what's bothering you."

5. The reading follows MS (S).

465 "My lord, since you've forgiven me,
I'll tell you—listen!
Once, in my great wickedness,
I spoke foolishly about my neighbor,
slandering her because she had twins.

470 I was really wronging myself.
The truth is, I then became pregnant
and had twin daughters; so I hid one,
had her abandoned in front of an abbey,
wrapped in our brocaded silk cloth,

475 wearing the ring that you gave me
when you first courted me.
I can't hide this from you:
I've found the ring and the cloth,
and also discovered our daughter,

480 whom I lost through my folly;
and this is she, right here,
the brave, wise, and beautiful girl
loved by the knight
who has married her sister."

485 Her husband said, "I'm delighted by this news;
I was never so pleased.
Since we've found our daughter,
God has given us great joy,
instead of doubling the sin.

490 My daughter," he said, "come here!"
The girl was overjoyed
by the story she'd heard.[6]
Her father won't wait any longer;
he goes to get his son-in-law,

495 and brings in the archbishop too—
he tells him the adventure.
When the knight heard the story
he was happier than he'd ever been.
The archbishop advised

6. "Story" renders *aventure*.

500   that things should be left as they were that night;
in the morning he would separate
the knight from the woman he had married.
They agreed to this plan.
Next morning, the marriage was annulled
505   and the knight married his beloved;
she was given to him by her father,
who was well disposed toward her;
he divided his inheritance with her.
The father and his wife remained at the festivities,
510   for as long as they lasted, with their daughter.
When they returned to their land,
they took their daughter Codre with them;
later, in their country,
she made a rich marriage too.
515   ✿ When this adventure became known
just as it happened,
the *lai* of Fresne was made from it.
It was named after its heroine.

✿ LE FRESNE (*The Ash Tree*)

VIRTUALLY ALL readers of Marie's *lais* agree on the charm and
effectiveness of *Le Fresne*. Its adroit combination of three
durable motifs in European folktale and fiction pays tribute to
Marie's craftsmanship as a storyteller, for the interaction among
the three elements of the plot is as unforced as it is dramatic.
The first motif is the romance of a heroine (or hero) who is
abandoned, in infancy, by her noble parents, is found and
raised by benevolent foster parents, and who then falls in love,
only to be threatened with the loss of her beloved to a rival of
higher rank. The protagonist's true station in life is discovered
at the last minute, thanks to the identification of tokens left

in her possession when she was abandoned, and the story ends with a double "recovery"—marriage to the beloved and reconciliation with the repentant parents. (A popular version of this plot is embodied in the Greek romance *Daphnis and Chloe.*) In the second of Marie's plot motifs, a wicked woman who falsely accuses another of a crime is placed by fortune in the position of appearing to have committed the same crime. To protect herself (or as a punishment) she loses her child, and years later, when she accidentally finds the child again, is impelled to repentance and confession, thereby winning the right to keep her offspring. The final motif of *Fresne* is the female Job or patient Griselda, as she is called in the later medieval versions of Boccaccio, Petrarch, and Chaucer. A young woman of low rank is chosen by a nobleman as his consort; her devotion is severely tested by the husband or by fortune, but she remains faithful in adversity and her virtue is suitably recognized at the story's happy ending.

In *Le Fresne,* the heroine's growth from helpless infant-foundling to a young woman of great beauty and moral stature provides her circular journey away from and back to her parents with a strong element of progress;[1] it imparts to the fortuitous events of the conclusion a moral force and, above all, permits a seamless joining of the three plot elements. At the beginning of the story, Fresne's mother slanderously accuses a neighbor of adultery for bearing twin children (according to the popular belief that two children in one birth point to two fathers); when she herself bears twins, she realizes she has brought about her own disgrace. Since she prefers offending God to shaming herself, she prepares to murder one of the children. She is dissuaded by one of her damsels, who volunteers instead to leave the child at the gate of a monastery (a not uncommon fate for unwanted children in the Middle Ages), where it will receive a good upbringing without bringing grief to its mother.

The selfless offer of the *meschine,* the girl, which saves Fresne's life and her mother's reputation, embodies a mature, deeply moral response to life's chances and human relationships: having been nurtured by her mistress, who has loved and cherished her, the girl is now in a position to repay that earlier protection with a reciprocal manifestation of love at the moment when it will do her lady the most good. Her gesture prefigures Fresne's crucial response of selfless devotion to her lord, Gurun, out of gratitude for his love. Even though Gurun is about to marry Codre and abandon Fresne, Fresne, to dignify it, places her prized possession, the luxurious coverlet in which she was wrapped by her mother, on the nuptial bed of Gurun and Codre. By this gesture, Fresne makes possible her mother's discovery of her identity and thus brings about the *lai*'s double denouement: the mother confesses her sin to her husband and receives her lost daughter back into the family, and Fresne, her noble lineage thus revealed, recovers Gurun in marriage.

The symbolic act of covering the bed of her apparently faithless lover is an emblem of Fresne's self-sacrifice, which, paradoxically, wins her back her full identity as daughter and as wife. It also stands as testimony to her capacity for love and action based on gratitude—an element of moral growth in her character that imposes linearity on the cycles of fortune in this romance. Finally, the placing of the swaddling robe on the marriage bed is an image of the continuity from generation to generation of the impulse to shelter those closest to us—and, ideally, all our fellow humans—in the protective envelope of love. This impulse to protect and nurture runs through the *lai*, exemplified not only by Fresne and the *meschine*, but by the abbess, and even by the old porter of the abbey who discovers the infant Fresne and brings her at once to his own widowed daughter so the infant can be nursed. (The juxtaposition of lost husband and found child suggests the rhythm of this romance world in which love and nurture must operate in order to give moral meaning to the cycle of death and birth.) Even Fresne's mother, in an earlier time, had nurtured the *meschine,* and the vassals who force Gurun to abandon Fresne for Codre (unknown to them, Fresne's sister) are moved by the desire that their lord have children who will assume his heritage and protect them from harm: i.e., be their feudal foster parents.

All these instances of nurture find their central symbol in the great shade tree that gives Fresne her name. Gurun's followers interpret Fresne's name in a negative sense, as a tree that, unlike the hazel (*la Codre*), bears no fruit; Marie, however, intends us to see the name proleptically: as the ash tree once protected its namesake, and as she has been nurtured by the abbess, so will she, in "protecting" Gurun with her mantle, establish her right to become his wife and the nurturer of his children.[2] Set in the midst of such a pervasive pattern, Fresne's mother's refusal to nurture her daughter at birth appears as a violation of the *lai*'s fundamental moral principle. Fortunately, in the optimistic world of *Le Fresne,* it is a breach that can be mended and repented at the right moment.

Marie encloses the main movement and theme of her miniature romance in a world of charming, sentimental details: the tableau of village sounds that tells the *meschine* she has come to the end of her search for a place to leave her infant charge; her prayer as she deposits the foundling in the tree; and the routine of the porter, interrupted by his discovery of the foundling. Marie's portrait of Gurun, the young lord who falls in love with Fresne without ever having seen her (cf. Equitan's similar passion from afar, and the troubadour tradition of distant love, *amor de lonh*) and later arranges to give large donations to the abbey as an excuse to see her regularly, is also affectionate and sentimental. His love for Fresne is pure and complete, and when he takes her away from the abbey to live with him as his mistress, Marie uses the same words to describe his treatment of her—*mut la cheri e mut l'ama*—that she has used to describe Fresne's mother's conduct toward the *meschine: et mut [l'ot] amee e mut cherie* ("and he [she] loved and cherished her much").

The harmony of plot motifs and (themes) endows *Le Fresne* with gemlike perfection, as Marie celebrates the triumph of protective love over the obstacles of human weakness, social circumstance, and fortune.

1. The interaction of circular and linear elements is a mark of the sophisticated romance plot. The element of movement away from and back to stasis (represented by a stable situation involving family ties, a well-defined social rank, or the like) reflects a perception of the cyclicality of human experience, often represented iconographically in the Middle Ages by the revolving wheel of fortune. The protagonist's endurance of this circular movement can coexist with an irreversible process of physical or moral growth, so that while he may seem merely to return to his starting point by the end of the romance, he has in fact become a very different person in the process, and therefore sees his old situation through new eyes, as it were.

2. On the significance of Fresne's name, see R. W. Hanning, "Uses of Names in Medieval Literature," *Names* 16 (1968), 337–338, and the article by Mickel on Marie's irony, cited in the bibliography.

Bisclavret (*The Werewolf*)

Since I am undertaking to compose *lais*,
I don't want to forget Bisclavret;
In Breton, the *lai*'s name is *Bisclavret*—
the Normans call it *Garwaf* [*The Werewolf*].
5 In the old days, people used to say—
and it often actually happened—
that some men turned into werewolves
and lived in the woods.
A werewolf is a savage beast;
10 while his fury is on him
he eats men, does much harm,
goes deep in the forest to live.
But that's enough of this for now:
I want to tell you about the Bisclavret.

15 ⚜ In Brittany there lived a nobleman
whom I've heard marvelously praised;
a fine, handsome knight
who behaved nobly.
He was close to his lord,
20 and loved by all his neighbors.
He had an estimable wife,
one of lovely appearance;
he loved her and she him,
but one thing was very vexing to her:
25 during the week he would be missing
for three whole days, and she didn't know
what happened to him or where he went.
Nor did any of his men know anything about it.
⚜ One day he returned home
30 happy and delighted;
she asked him about it.
"My lord," she said, "and dear love,
I'd very much like to ask you one thing—
if I dared;

92

35   but I'm so afraid of your anger
     that nothing frightens me more."
     When he heard that, he embraced her,
     drew her to him and kissed her.
     "My lady," he said, "go ahead and ask!
40   There's nothing you could want to know,
     that, if I knew the answer, I wouldn't tell you."
     "By God," she replied, "now I'm cured!
     My lord, on the days when you go away from me
     I'm in such a state—
45   so sad at heart,
     so afraid I'll lose you—
     that if I don't get quick relief
     I could die of this very soon.
     Please, tell me where you go,
50   where you have been staying.
     I think you must have a lover,
     and if that's so, you're doing wrong."
     "My dear," he said, "have mercy on me, for God's sake!
     Harm will come to me if I tell you about this,
55   because I'd lose your love
     and even my very self."
     When the lady heard this
     she didn't take it lightly;
     she kept asking him,
60   coaxed and flattered him so much,
     that he finally told her what happened to him—
     he hid nothing from her.
     "My dear, I become a werewolf:
     I go off into the great forest,
65   in the thickest part of the woods,
     and I live on the prey I hunt down."
     When he had told her everything,
     she asked further
     whether he undressed or kept his clothes on [when he became a
          werewolf].
70   "Wife," he replied, "I go stark naked."

"Tell me, then, for God's sake, where your clothes are."
"That I won't tell you;
for if I were to lose them,
and then be discovered,
75 I'd stay a werewolf forever.
I'd be helpless
until I got them back.
That's why I don't want their hiding place to be known."
"My lord," the lady answered,
80 "I love you more than all the world;
you mustn't hide anything from me
or fear me in any way:
that doesn't seem like love to me.
What wrong have I done? For what sin of mine
85 do you mistrust me about anything?
Do the right thing and tell me!"
She harassed and bedeviled him so,
that he had no choice but to tell her.
"Lady," he said, "near the woods,
90 beside the road that I use to get there,
there's an old chapel
that has often done me good service;
under a bush there is a big stone,
hollowed out inside;
95 I hide my clothes right there
until I'm ready to come home."
The lady heard this wonder
and turned scarlet from fear;
she was terrified of the whole adventure.
100 Over and over she considered
how she might get rid of him;
she never wanted to sleep with him again.
There was a knight of that region
who had loved her for a long time,
105 who begged for her love,
and dedicated himself to serving her.
She'd never loved him at all,

nor pledged her love to him,
but now she sent a messenger for him,
110 and told him her intention.
"My dear," she said, "cheer up!
I shall now grant you without delay
what you have suffered for;
you'll meet with no more refusals—
115 I offer you my love and my body;
make me your mistress!"
❧ He thanked her graciously
and accepted her promise,
and she bound him to her by an oath.
120 Then she told him
how her husband went away and what happened to him;
she also taught him the precise path
her husband took into the forest,
and then she sent the knight to get her husband's clothes.
125 So Bisclavret was betrayed,[1]
ruined by his own wife.
Since people knew he was often away from home
they all thought
this time he'd gone away forever.
130 They searched for him and made inquiries
but could never find him,
so they had to let matters stand.
The wife later married the other knight,
who had loved her for so long.
135 ❧ A whole year passed
until one day the king went hunting;
he headed right for the forest
where Bisclavret was.
When the hounds were unleashed,
140 they ran across Bisclavret;
the hunters and the dogs
chased him all day,

---

1. Hereafter Bisclavret will be treated as a proper name, and the definite article omitted.

until they were just about to take him
and tear him apart,
145 at which point he saw the king
and ran to him, pleading for mercy.
He took hold of the king's stirrup,
kissed his leg and his foot.
The king saw this and was terrified;
150 he called his companions.
"My lords," he said, "come quickly!
Look at this marvel—
this beast is humbling itself to me.
It has the mind of a man, and it's begging me for mercy!
155 Chase the dogs away,
and make sure no one strikes it.
This beast is rational—he has a mind.
Hurry up: let's get out of here.
I'll extend my peace to the creature;
160 indeed, I'll hunt no more today!"
Thereupon the king turned away.
Bisclavret followed him;
he stayed close to the king, and wouldn't go away;
he'd no intention of leaving him.
165 〽 The king led him to his castle;
he was delighted with this turn of events,
for he'd never seen anything like it.
He considered the beast a great wonder
and held him very dear.
170 He commanded all his followers,
for the sake of their love for him, to guard Bisclavret well,
and under no circumstances to do him harm;
none of them should strike him;
rather, he should be well fed and watered.
175 They willingly guarded the creature;
every day he went to sleep
among the knights, near the king.
Everyone was fond of him;
he was so noble and well behaved

180 that he never wished to do anything wrong.
     Regardless of where the king might go,
     Bisclavret never wanted to be separated from him;
     he always accompanied the king.
     The king became very much aware that the creature loved him.
185 🦋 Now listen to what happened next.
     The king held a court;
     to help him celebrate his feast
     and to serve him as handsomely as possible,
     he summoned all the barons
190 who held fiefs from him.
     Among the knights who went,
     and all dressed up in his best attire,
     was the one who had married Bisclavret's wife.
     He neither knew nor suspected
195 that he would find Bisclavret so close by.
     As soon as he came to the palace
     Bisclavret saw him,
     ran toward him at full speed,
     sank his teeth into him, and started to drag him down.
200 He would have done him great damage
     if the king hadn't called him off,
     and threatened him with a stick.
     Twice that day he tried to bite the knight.
     Everyone was extremely surprised,
205 since the beast had never acted that way
     toward any other man he had seen.
     All over the palace people said
     that he wouldn't act that way without a reason:
     that somehow or other, the knight had mistreated Bisclavret,
210 and now he wanted his revenge.
     And so the matter rested
     until the feast was over
     and until the barons took their leave of the king
     and started home.
215 The very first to leave,
     to the best of my knowledge,

was the knight whom Bisclavret had attacked.
It's no wonder the creature hated him.
𝕏𝕤𝕤 Not long afterward,
220 as the story leads me to believe,
the king, who was so wise and noble,
went back to the forest
where he had found Bisclavret,
and the creature went with him.
225 That night, when he finished hunting,
he sought lodging out in the countryside.
The wife of Bisclavret heard about it,
dressed herself elegantly,
and went the next day to speak with the king,
230 bringing rich presents for him.
When Bisclavret saw her coming,
no one could hold him back;
he ran toward her in a rage.
Now listen to how well he avenged himself!
235 He tore the nose off her face.
What worse thing could he have done to her?
Now men closed in on him from all sides;
they were about to tear him apart,
when a wise man said to the king,
240 "My lord, listen to me!
This beast has stayed with you,
and there's not one of us
who hasn't watched him closely,
hasn't traveled with him often.
245 He's never touched anyone,
or shown any wickedness,
except to this woman.
By the faith that I owe you,
he has some grudge against her,
250 and against her husband as well.
This is the wife of the knight
whom you used to like so much,

and who's been missing for so long—
we don't know what became of him.
255 Why not put this woman to torture
and see if she'll tell you
why the beast hates her?
Make her tell what she knows!
We've seen many strange things
260 happen in Brittany!"
    The king took his advice;
he detained the knight.
At the same time he took the wife
and subjected her to torture;
265 out of fear and pain
she told all about her husband:
how she had betrayed him
and taken away his clothes;
the story he had told her
270 about what happened to him and where he went;
and how after she had taken his clothes
he'd never been seen in his land again.
She was quite certain
that this beast was Bisclavret.
275 The king demanded the clothes;
whether she wanted to or not
she sent home for them,
and had them brought to Bisclavret.
When they were put down in front of him
280 he didn't even seem to notice them;
the king's wise man—
the one who had advised him earlier—
said to him, "My lord, you're not doing it right.
This beast wouldn't, under any circumstances,
285 in order to get rid of his animal form,
put on his clothes in front of you;
you don't understand what this means:
he's just too ashamed to do it here.
Have him led to your chambers

290 and bring the clothes with him;
    then we'll leave him alone for a while.
    If he turns into a man, we'll know about it."
    ⚜ The king himself led the way
    and closed all the doors on him.
295 After a while he went back,
    taking two barons with him;
    all three entered the king's chamber.
    On the king's royal bed
    they found the knight asleep.
300 The king ran to embrace him.
    He hugged and kissed him again and again.
    As soon as he had the chance,
    the king gave him back all his lands;
    he gave him more than I can tell.
305 He banished the wife,
    chased her out of the country.
    She went into exile with the knight
    with whom she had betrayed her lord.
    She had several children
310 who were widely known
    for their appearance:
    several women of the family
    were actually born without noses,
    and lived out their lives noseless.

315 ⚜ The adventure that you have heard
    really happened, no doubt about it.
    The *lai* of Bisclavret was made
    so it would be remembered forever.

⚜ BISCLAVRET *(The Werewolf)*

In *Bisclavret*, Marie turns to the folklore of lycanthropy—
a subject of deep fascination for European culture. Antecedents

of Marie's story include versions in Pliny's *Historia naturalis* and Petronius' *Satyricon;* her version seems in turn to have influenced episodes in the later medieval *Lai de Melion* and *Roman de Renart le Contrefait.* In Marie's hands, the story of the man compelled by fortune (*aventure*) to spend part of his existence as a beast of prey in the forest becomes a parable about the forces of bestiality that exist within human nature and how they should (and should not) be confronted, used, or transcended. None of the *lais* is more deeply concerned with the fragility of social existence, given the battle within men and women between their higher and baser impulses, but *Bisclavret* is also concerned with the human capacity to manifest nobility even under the most trying conditions, and thus to transcend the animal part of our nature and garner the hard-won benefits of civilization.

Marie plays upon and reverses our expectations in the exposition of *Bisclavret,* so that, unlike the case in *Equitan* (for example), the moral point of the story only gradually emerges from its twistings and turnings and is never pressed overtly upon us. The effect of this technique is to establish a parallel between Bisclavret's *aventure*—his fall into and then rescue from bestial shape—and the audience's struggle to free itself from its initial misapprehensions and attain a clear understanding of the significance of the werewolf's emblematic career.

The *lai* opens with a word picture of the werewolf, stressing his man-eating brutality. (Ironically, the closest the protagonist will come to such behavior is biting off his disloyal wife's nose, a gesture of justifiable revenge rather than of uncontrolled savagery.) This evocation of the werewolf as the beast that lurks within a man and breaks out periodically prompts our initial sympathy with the wife's reaction of fear and loathing when she learns that her husband is such a creature—a reaction that leads her to betray him in her desire to escape.

Yet Marie also makes it clear that the protagonist, in his human phase, is noble, a trusted companion of his lord, and a man beloved of his neighbors. His one failing, aside from the lycanthropy that is beyond his control, is his inability to keep his secret from his wife, although he knows that his confession, in response to her entreaties, may well cause him to lose her, and his human shape, forever. He loves not wisely but too well; she, on the other hand, does not love, or trust, enough. Faced with the dark side of her husband's nature, she forgets all his virtues, as enumerated by Marie in the passage cited above, and desperately arranges to free herself by a double betrayal. She accepts the favors of a suitor she has hitherto scorned, and exploits his desire to serve her by instructing him to steal the werewolf's hidden clothes, thereby preventing his return to his human shape. Her husband thus disposed of, she marries the suitor.

By this point, our original responses to the werewolf and his wife have undergone a transformation to sympathy for the betrayed man-beast and disapproval, if not disgust, for the wife. Marie's intention has also emerged: the werewolf is an image of human nature, capable of nobility, but also of irrationality and bestiality. His wife sees him only through a self-centered haze of idealizing love; her main worry about his absences is that he is betraying her with another woman, which is another irony, considering her subsequent behavior. His revelation of the full ambiguities of his nature, far from prompting sympathy and aid, sends her reeling, unable to face the truth. Her absolute love turns at once to absolute loathing; she can now see only his bestial side (though it has never harmed her), and, seeking to destroy this knowledge that has contaminated her vision of life, she turns to another man who has wooed her in the ideal manner of stereotypical, troubadour-like courtly love. She takes refuge in this partial vision and, in fact, uses it to put the now blighted husband out of her life and sight forever. The wife's failure of trust results from her obsession with her husband's potential for evil; her abandonment of him, with the theft of his clothes, is thus a self-fulfilling prophecy, imprisoning him forever (as it seems) within the bestial self she so fears. The wife's treason and the loss of the werewolf's clothing are reciprocal metaphors; both embody a loss of that civilizing force in life—symbolized at the surface level by apparel, at a deeper level by the love relationship—which saves humanity from perpetual servitude to its lower, amoral impulses, and allows it to engage in the satisfying social relationships enumerated in Marie's opening statement about the protagonist.

The victimization of the man-beast is not, however, the end of the story; more reversals are in store. The werewolf is discovered by the king he served in human form, while the latter is out hunting. When the beast makes motions of obeisance and begs for mercy, the king, despite initial fear, recognizes human awareness (*sen de hume*) in the creature, and saves him from the hunting dogs. In this scene, the narrative, which till now has presented the human condition as the beast that lurks within man (and woman, for the wife's fear and disloyalty are equally "bestial"), asks us to look anew at that condition and discover the man that lurks within the beast, to wit, the potential for graceful ingenuity in adversity manifested by the werewolf, and for mercy in the face of fear manifested by the king (though not the wife). The werewolf answers the king's compassion with further civilized behavior: he becomes the king's inseparable companion and acts nobly to all the courtiers, who recognize his love for the king who has saved him (another implied comment on the wife).

Only when the werewolf encounters his wife's new husband, and then the wife herself, does he behave "bestially," by attacking them. But a perceptive courtier (yet another foil to the imperceptive wife) realizes there must be a reason for this departure from the creature's normal behavior; by putting the savagery into perspective, the court recognizes that the werewolf can make moral distinctions between good and bad, friend and foe. This moral awareness allows him to channel his capacity for violence into the appropriate, civilized punishment of evil. By this demonstration of his powers of discrimination, the werewolf wins the chance to recover his human form: the king, following his councillor's advice, forces a confession from the wife, and forces her to produce her husband's clothes as well. As the wife's betrayal was metaphorically linked to the husband's loss of his clothing and thus his human shape, so now does his recovery of them follow on, and express metaphorically, his reintegration back into a human community founded on the perception, compassion, and love shown to him by the king and his court.

Before his final metamorphosis, the werewolf demonstrates a final civilized virtue, shame: he refuses to don his clothes in public. This reticence, which the councillor sympathetically understands but which probably strikes us as amusing, if not absurd, has a double significance. First, the cultivation of shame—the unwillingness to fall below a certain level of behavior in the presence of one's peers—is a mark of human social awareness, of sensitivity to others. Second, the werewolf's reluctance to let others see him changing his form reverses his foolish willingness to reveal this shape-shifting to his wife at the beginning of the *lai*. He has, in effect, learned his lesson about the need for privacy, and thus fully deserves to return to full humanity and social integration.

Thus the king, by his trust in the man-in-beast, wins back a noble vassal; his human treatment of the werewolf is another self-fulfilling prophecy, while the wife sees her prophetic fear of the beast-in-man come true in becoming the victim of the werewolf's only bestial deed (the loss of her nose). In *Bisclavret,* Marie argues that human beings are defined not only by their inherent potential for good or evil but also by their fellow humans' responses of trust or fear to that potential. Thus love is lauded as a socializing force in the *lai,* and its betrayal condemned as the ultimate antisocial act.

Lanval

I shall tell you the adventure of another *lai,*
just as it happened:
it was composed about a very noble vassal;
in Breton, they call him Lanval.

5   Arthur, the brave and the courtly king,
was staying at Cardoel,
because the Scots and the Picts
were destroying the land.
They invaded Logres[1]
10 and laid it waste.
At Pentecost, in summer,[2]
the king stayed there.
He gave out many rich gifts:
to counts and barons,
15 members of the Round Table—
such a company had no equal[3] in all the world—
he distributed wives and lands,
to all but one who had served him.
That was Lanval; Arthur forgot him,
20 and none of his men favored him either.
For his valor, for his generosity,
his beauty and his bravery,
most men envied him;
some feigned the appearance of love
25 who, if something unpleasant happened to him,
would not have been at all disturbed.
He was the son of a king of high degree

---

1. Logres is England.

2. In medieval poetry, only two seasons are usually recognized, summer
and winter. The feast of Pentecost is frequently the starting point of an
Arthurian adventure.

3. Equal in number as well as in worth: cf. Ewert, "There was no equal
number of such knights in all the world" (p. 173).

but he was far from his heritage.
He was of the king's household
30 but he had spent all his wealth,
for the king gave him nothing
nor did Lanval ask.
Now Lanval was in difficulty,
depressed and very worried.
35 My lords, don't be surprised:
a strange man, without friends,
is very sad in another land,
when he doesn't know where to look for help.
The knight of whom I speak,
40 who had served the king so long,
one day mounted his horse
and went off to amuse himself.
He left the city
and came, all alone, to a field;
45 he dismounted by a running stream
but his horse trembled badly.
He removed the saddle and went off,
leaving the horse to roll around in the meadow.
He folded his cloak beneath his head
50 and lay down.
He worried about his difficulty,
he could see nothing that pleased him.
As he lay there
he looked down along the bank
55 and saw two girls approaching;
he had never seen any lovelier.
They were richly dressed,
tightly laced,
in tunics of dark purple;
60 their faces were very lovely.
The older one carried basins,
golden, well made, and fine;
I shall tell you the truth about it, without fail.
The other carried a towel.

65 They went straight
   to where the knight was lying.
   Lanval, who was very well bred,
   got up to meet them.
   They greeted him first
70 and gave him their message:
   "Sir Lanval, my lady,
   who is worthy and wise and beautiful,
   sent us for you.
   Come with us now.
75 We shall guide you there safely.
   See, her pavilion is nearby!"
   The knight went with them;
   giving no thought to his horse
   who was feeding before him in the meadow.
80 They led him up to the tent,
   which was quite beautiful and well placed.
   Queen Semiramis,
   however much more wealth,
   power, or knowledge she had,
85 or the emperor Octavian
   could not have paid for one of the flaps.
   There was a golden eagle on top of it,
   whose value I could not tell,
   nor could I judge the value of the cords or the poles
90 that held up the sides of the tent;
   there is no king on earth who could buy it,
   no matter what wealth he offered.
   The girl was inside the tent:
   the lily and the young rose
95 when they appear in the summer
   are surpassed by her beauty.
   She lay on a beautiful bed—
   the bedclothes were worth a castle—
   dressed only in her shift.
100 Her body was well shaped and elegant;
   for the heat, she had thrown over herself,

     a precious cloak of white ermine,
     covered with purple alexandrine,
     but her whole side was uncovered,
105 her face, her neck and her bosom;
     she was whiter than the hawthorn flower.
     The knight went forward
     and the girl addressed him.
     He sat before the bed.
110 "Lanval," she said, "sweet love,
     because of you I have come from my land;
     I came to seek you from far away.
     If you are brave and courtly,
     no emperor or count or king
115 will ever have known such joy or good;
     for I love you more than anything."
     He looked at her and saw that she was beautiful;
     Love stung him with a spark
     that burned and set fire to his heart.
120 He answered her in a suitable way.
     "Lovely one," he said, "if it pleased you,
     if such joy might be mine
     that you would love me,
     there is nothing you might command,
125 within my power, that I would not do,
     whether foolish or wise.
     I shall obey your command;
     for you, I shall abandon everyone.
     I want never to leave you.
130 That is what I most desire."
     When the girl heard the words
     of the man who could love her so,
     she granted him her love and her body.
     Now Lanval was on the right road!
135 Afterward, she gave him a gift:
     he would never again want anything,
     he would receive as he desired;

however generously he might give and spend,
she would provide what he needed.
140 Now Lanval is well cared for.
The more lavishly he spends,
the more gold and silver he will have.
"Love," she said, "I admonish you now,
I command and beg you,
145 do not let any man know about this.
I shall tell you why:
you would lose me for good
if this love were known;
you would never see me again
150 or possess my body."
He answered that he would do
exactly as she commanded.
He lay beside her on the bed;
now Lanval is well cared for.
155 He remained with her
that afternoon, until evening
and would have stayed longer, if he could,
and if his love had consented.
"Love," she said, "get up.
160 You cannot stay any longer.
Go away now; I shall remain
but I will tell you one thing:
when you want to talk to me
there is no place you can think of
165 where a man might have his mistress
without reproach or shame,
that I shall not be there with you
to satisfy all your desires.
No man but you will see me
170 or hear my words."
When he heard her, he was very happy,
he kissed her, and then got up.
The girls who had brought him to the tent
dressed him in rich clothes;

175 when he was dressed anew,
there wasn't a more handsome youth in all the world;
he was no fool, no boor.
They gave him water for his hands
and a towel to dry them,
180 and they brought him food.
He took supper with his love;
it was not to be refused.
He was served with great courtesy,
he received it with great joy.
185 There was an entremet
that vastly pleased the knight
for he kissed his lady often
and held her close.
When they finished dinner,
190 his horse was brought to him.
The horse had been well saddled;
Lanval was very richly served.
The knight took his leave, mounted,
and rode toward the city,
195 often looking behind him.
Lanval was very disturbed;
he wondered about his adventure
and was doubtful in his heart;
he was amazed, not knowing what to believe;
200 he didn't expect ever to see her again.
He came to his lodging
and found his men well dressed.
That night, his accommodations were rich
but no one knew where it came from.
205 There was no knight in the city
who really needed a place to stay
whom he didn't invite to join him
to be well and richly served.
Lanval gave rich gifts,
210 Lanval released prisoners,

Lanval dressed jongleurs [performers],
Lanval offered great honors.
There was no stranger or friend
to whom Lanval didn't give.
215 Lanval's joy and pleasure were intense;
in the daytime or at night,
he could see his love often;
she was completely at his command.

In that same year, it seems to me,
220 after the feast of St. John,
about thirty knights
were amusing themselves
in an orchard beneath the tower
where the queen was staying.
225 Gawain was with them
and his cousin, the handsome Yvain;
Gawain, the noble, the brave,
who was so loved by all, said:
"By God, my lords, we wronged
230 our companion Lanval,
who is so generous and courtly,
and whose father is a rich king,
when we didn't bring him with us."
They immediately turned back,
235 went to his lodging
and prevailed on Lanval to come along with them.
At a sculpted window
the queen was looking out;
she had three ladies with her.
240 She saw the king's retinue,
recognized Lanval and looked at him.
Then she told one of her ladies
to send for her maidens,
the loveliest and the most refined;
245 together they went to amuse themselves

in the orchard where the others were.
She brought thirty or more with her;
they descended the steps.
The knights came to meet them,
250 because they were delighted to see them.
The knights took them by the hand;
their conversation was in no way vulgar.
Lanval went off to one side,
far from the others; he was impatient
255 to hold his love,
to kiss and embrace and touch her;
he thought little of others' joys
if he could not have his pleasure.
When the queen saw him alone,
260 she went straight to the knight.
She sat beside him and spoke,
revealing her whole heart:
"Lanval, I have shown you much honor,
I have cherished you, and loved you.
265 You may have all my love;
just tell me your desire.
I promise you my affection.
You should be very happy with me."
"My lady," he said, "let me be!
270 I have no desire to love you.
I've served the king a long time;
I don't want to betray my faith to him.
Never, for you or for your love,
will I do anything to harm my lord."
275 The queen got angry;
in her wrath, she insulted him:
"Lanval," she said, "I am sure
you don't care for such pleasure;
people have often told me
280 that you have no interest in women.
You have fine-looking boys
with whom you enjoy yourself.

Base coward, lousy cripple,
my lord made a bad mistake
285 when he let you stay with him.
For all I know, he'll lose God because of it."
When Lanval heard her, he was quite disturbed;
he was not slow to answer.
He said something out of spite
290 that he would later regret.
"Lady," he said, "of that activity
I know nothing,
but I love and I am loved
by one who should have the prize
295 over all the women I know.
And I shall tell you one thing;
you might as well know all:
any one of those who serve her,
the poorest girl of all,
300 is better than you, my lady queen,
in body, face, and beauty,
in breeding and in goodness."
The queen left him
and went, weeping, to her chamber.
305 She was upset and angry
because he had insulted her.
She went to bed sick;
never, she said, would she get up
unless the king gave her satisfaction
310 for the offense against her.
The king returned from the woods,
he'd had a very good day.
He entered the queen's chambers.
When she saw him, she began to complain.
315 She fell at his feet, asked his mercy,
saying that Lanval had dishonored her;
he had asked for her love,
and because she refused him
he insulted and offended her:

320　he boasted of a love
　　　who was so refined and noble and proud
　　　that her chambermaid,
　　　the poorest one who served her,
　　　was better than the queen.
325　The king got very angry;
　　　he swore an oath:
　　　if Lanval could not defend himself in court
　　　he would have him burned or hanged.
　　　The king left her chamber
330　and called for three of his barons;
　　　he sent them for Lanval
　　　who was feeling great sorrow and distress.
　　　He had come back to his dwelling,
　　　knowing very well
335　that he'd lost his love,
　　　he had betrayed their affair.
　　　He was all alone in a room,
　　　disturbed and troubled;
　　　he called on his love, again and again,
340　but it did him no good.
　　　He complained and sighed,
　　　from time to time he fainted;
　　　then he cried a hundred times for her to have mercy
　　　and speak to her love.
345　He cursed his heart and his mouth;
　　　it's a wonder he didn't kill himself.
　　　No matter how much he cried and shouted,
　　　ranted and raged,
　　　she would not have mercy on him,
350　not even let him see her.
　　　How will he ever contain himself?
　　　The men the king sent
　　　arrived and told him
　　　to appear in court without delay:
355　the king had summoned him

because the queen had accused him.
Lanval went with his great sorrow;
they could have killed him, for all he cared.
He came before the king;
360 he was very sad, thoughtful, silent;
his face revealed great suffering.
In anger the king told him:
"Vassal, you have done me a great wrong!
This was a base undertaking,
365 to shame and disgrace me
and to insult the queen.
You have made a foolish boast:
your love is much too noble
if her maid is more beautiful,
370 more worthy, than the queen."
Lanval denied that he'd dishonored
or shamed his lord,
word for word, as the king spoke:
he had not made advances to the queen;
375 but of what he had said,
he acknowledged the truth,
about the love he had boasted of,
that now made him sad because he'd lost her.
About that he said he would do
380 whatever the court decided.
The king was very angry with him;
he sent for all his men
to determine exactly what he ought to do
so that no one could find fault with his decision.
385 They did as he commanded,
whether they liked it or not.
They assembled,
judged, and decided,
than Lanval should have his day;
390 but he must find pledges for his lord
to guarantee that he would await the judgment,

return, and be present at it.
Then the court would be increased,
for now there were none but the king's household.
395 The barons came back to the king
and announced their decision.
The king demanded pledges.
Lanval was alone and forlorn,
he had no relative, no friend.
400 Gawain went and pledged himself for him,
and all his companions followed.
The king addressed them: "I release him to you
on forfeit of whatever you hold from me,
lands and fiefs, each one for himself."
405 When Lanval was pledged, there was nothing else to do.
He returned to his lodging.
The knights accompanied him,
they reproached and admonished him
that he give up his great sorrow;
410 they cursed his foolish love.
Each day they went to see him,
because they wanted to know
whether he was drinking and eating;
they were afraid that he'd kill himself.
415 On the day that they had named,
the barons assembled.
The king and the queen were there
and the pledges brought Lanval back.
They were all very sad for him:
420 I think there were a hundred
who would have done all they could
to set him free without a trial
where he would be wrongly accused.
The king demanded a verdict
425 according to the charge and rebuttal.
Now it all fell to the barons.
They went to the judgment,
worried and distressed

for the noble man from another land
430 who'd gotten into such trouble in their midst.
Many wanted to condemn him
in order to satisfy their lord.
The Duke of Cornwall said:
"No one can blame us;
435 whether it makes you weep or sing
justice must be carried out.
The king spoke against his vassal
whom I have heard named Lanval;
he accused him of felony,
440 charged him with a misdeed—
a love that he had boasted of,
which made the queen angry.
No one but the king accused him:
by the faith I owe you,
445 if one were to speak the truth,
there should have been no need for defense,
except that a man owes his lord honor
in every circumstance.
He will be bound by his oath,
450 and the king will forgive us our pledges
if he can produce proof;
if his love would come forward,
if what he said,
what upset the queen, is true,
455 then he will be acquitted,
because he did not say it out of malice.
But if he cannot get his proof,
we must make it clear to him
that he will forfeit his service to the king;
460 he must take his leave."
They sent to the knight,
told and announced to him
that he should have his love come
to defend and stand surety for him.
465 He told them that he could not do it:

he would never receive help from her.
They went back to the judges,
not expecting any help from Lanval.
The king pressed them hard
470 because of the queen who was waiting.
When they were ready to give their verdict
they saw two girls approaching,
riding handsome palfreys.
They were very attractive,
475 dressed in purple taffeta,
over their bare skin.
The men looked at them with pleasure.
Gawain, taking three knights with him,
went to Lanval and told him;
480 he pointed out the two girls.
Gawain was extremely happy, and begged him
to tell if his love were one of them.
Lanval said he didn't know who they were,
where they came from or where they were going.
485 The girls proceeded
still on horseback;
they dismounted before the high table
at which Arthur, the king, sat.
They were of great beauty,
490 and spoke in a courtly manner:
"King, clear your chambers,
have them hung with silk
where my lady may dismount;
she wishes to take shelter with you."
495 He promised it willingly
and called two knights
to guide them up to the chambers.
On that subject no more was said.
The king asked his barons
500 for their judgment and decision;
he said they had angered him very much
with their long delay.

"Sire," they said, "we have decided.
Because of the ladies we have just seen
505 we have made no judgment.
Let us reconvene the trial."
Then they assembled, everyone was worried;
there was much noise and strife.
While they were in that confusion,
510 two girls in noble array,
dressed in Phrygian silks
and riding Spanish mules,
were seen coming down the street.
This gave the vassals great joy;
515 to each other they said that now
Lanval, the brave and bold, was saved.
Gawain went up to him,[4]
bringing his companions along.
"Sire," he said, "take heart.
520 For the love of God, speak to us.
Here come two maidens,
well adorned and very beautiful;
one must certainly be your love."
Lanval answered quickly
525 that he did not recognize them,
he didn't know them or love them.
Meanwhile they'd arrived,
and dismounted before the king.
Most of those who saw them praised them
530 for their bodies, their faces, their coloring;
each was more impressive
than the queen had ever been.
The older one was courtly and wise,
she spoke her message fittingly:
535 "King, have chambers prepared for us
to lodge my lady according to her need;

---

4. Ewert gives Yweins; Warnke, Walwains. Gawain seems more likely, since
he is the one most concerned with Lanval throughout and since he always
moves with his companions, as in this case.

she is coming here to speak with you."
He ordered them to be taken
to the others who had preceded them.
540 There was no problem with the mules.[5]
When he had seen to the girls,
he summoned all his barons
to render their judgment;
it had already dragged out too much.
545 The queen was getting angry
because she had fasted so long.[6]
They were about to give their judgment
when through the city came riding
a girl on horseback:
550 there was none more beautiful in the world.
She rode a white palfrey,
who carried her handsomely and smoothly:
he was well apportioned in the neck and head,
no finer beast in the world.
555 The palfrey's trappings were rich;
under heaven there was no count or king
who could have afforded them all
without selling or mortgaging lands.
She was dressed in this fashion:
560 in a white linen shift
that revealed both her sides
since the lacing was along the side.
Her body was elegant, her hips slim,
her neck whiter than snow on a branch,
565 her eyes bright, her face white,
a beautiful mouth, a well-set nose,
dark eyebrows and an elegant forehead,
her hair curly and rather blond;
golden wire does not shine

5. The following two lines are added in (S) to explain this remark: "There
were enough men to care for them / and put them into the stables."

6. Warnke and Rychner give *jeünot*; Ewert, *atendeit*, "waited," which is not
quite as callously selfish.

570 like her hair in the light.
 Her cloak, which she had wrapped around her,
 was dark purple.
 On her wrist she held a sparrow hawk,
 a greyhound followed her.[7]

575 In the town, no one, small or big,
 old man or child,
 failed to come look.
 As they watched her pass,
 there was no joking about her beauty.

580 She proceeded at a slow pace.
 The judges who saw her
 marveled at the sight;
 no one who looked at her
 was not warmed with joy.

585 Those who loved the knight
 came to him and told him
 of the girl who was approaching,
 if God pleased, to rescue him.
 "Sir companion, here comes one

590 neither tawny nor dark;
 this is, of all who exist,
 the most beautiful woman in the world."
 Lanval heard them and lifted his head;
 he recognized her and sighed.

595 The blood rose to his face;
 he was quick to speak.
 "By my faith," he said, "that is my love.
 Now I don't care if I am killed,
 if only she forgives me.

600 For I am restored, now that I see her."
 The lady entered the palace;
 no one so beautiful had ever been there.

---

7. (S) adds the following attractive if doubtful lines: "A noble youth led her / carrying an ivory horn. / They came through the street, very beautiful. / Such great beauty was not seen / in Venus, who was a queen, / or in Dido, or in Lavinia."

She dismounted before the king
so that she was well seen by all.

605 And she let her cloak fall
so they could see her better.
The king, who was well bred,
rose and went to meet her;
all the others honored her

610 and offered to serve her.
When they had looked at her well,
when they had greatly praised her beauty,
she spoke in this way,
she didn't want to wait:

615 "I have loved one of your vassals:
you see him before you—Lanval.
He has been accused in your court—
I don't want him to suffer
for what he said; you should know

620 that the queen was in the wrong.
He never made advances to her.
And for the boast that he made,
if he can be acquitted through me,
let him be set free by your barons."

625 Whatever the barons judged by law
the king promised would prevail.
To the last man they agreed
that Lanval had successfully answered the charge.
He was set free by their decision

630 and the girl departed.
The king could not detain her,
though there were enough people to serve her.
Outside the hall stood
a great stone of dark marble

635 where heavy men mounted
when they left the king's court;
Lanval climbed on it.
When the girl came through the gate
Lanval leapt, in one bound,

640 onto the palfrey, behind her.
With her he went to Avalun,
so the Bretons tell us,
to a very beautiful island;
there the youth was carried off.
645 No man heard of him again,
and I have no more to tell.

🌸 LANVAL

IN THIS *lai,* Marie presents a contrast between the world which
love enables lovers to create for themselves and the world of
ordinary human society, where they must otherwise live. The
world of love is complete in itself; secular society, even in its
noblest form, the Arthurian court, is shown to be severely
limited. The hero is mistreated at Arthur's court, despite his
valuable service to the king and his generous spending of his
fortune. The king forgets him when he distributes wives and
lands, and other knights envy him. A stranger in Arthur's
land, Lanval is further isolated by the neglect of the court,
which forces him to turn inward. He goes off alone and finds
or imagines a love that gives him all that he lacked in the
world and more.

Like the bird-knight who comes to the imprisoned lady in
Yonec, Lanval's love comes to him because he needs her and
whenever he needs her, but she remains invisible to everyone
else, as though she were the creation of his fantasy. Indeed,
even when she does appear to the court at the end of the *lai,*
she is the climax of a wonderful and otherworldly procession of
beauty and wealth. Her rich clothes and trappings, the hawk
and the hunting dog, suggest an allegorical figure, a personifica-
tion of Love, and all who see her perceive her as their ideal
beauty. She offers Lanval enormous wealth, enabling him to
help others, but he is concerned only with her love. Her beauty

is never described without reference to her fabulous wealth; Arthur's world is impressed with both, Lanval only with her.

Ironically, love gives him the means to win attention at court, but it also destroys his interest in such attention. Henceforth he chooses to keep himself apart from others so that he can think about his love, and the others must seek him out. Lanval's desire to be alone provides another contrast with the Arthurian world, where fellowship was valued, a point Marie underlines rather humorously by having Gawain take two or three companions wherever he goes. But now, when Lanval would be happier by himself, he is not left alone. Love seems also to make him more attractive to others and even the queen begins to make advances to him. This puts the hero in a difficult predicament: he must reject the queen out of loyalty to his love, but his rejection offends her and she insults him. Her insults provoke him to boast about his love and in so doing he betrays his vow of secrecy and thus forfeits the love.

As in so many of Marie's *lais* (cf. *Yonec, Laustic*), once the love is known to others it is lost, as though it can only exist as the private possession of the lovers and is somehow demeaned when brought into contact with the outside world. But in contrast to *Yonec* and *Laustic*, Marie permits the love to triumph in this *lai*. The lady returns to rescue Lanval despite his betrayal of their secret, because his love for her has not wavered. His only concern when he is accused is that he has lost her—his disgrace at court does not trouble him at all. Her mercy, despite his fault, is in sharp contrast to the king's attempt to condemn Lanval for an act he did not commit.

The superficiality, perhaps even falseness, of the court's values, which was apparent in the mistreatment of Lanval at the beginning, is revealed particularly in the accusation and trial of the hero. The queen, offended by his rejection, first accuses him of homosexuality, a conclusion the court has leapt to because he takes no interest in women there. When that is answered by Lanval's boast about the superior beauty of his love and of the least of her servants over the queen's, the queen takes revenge, like Potiphar's wife, and accuses Lanval of trying to make love to her. The contrast between the pettiness, the vulgarity, and the immorality of the queen and the perfection of the woman Lanval loves is obvious. The queen's charge causes the king to accuse Lanval, publicly, of wronging him, although Lanval had protested his loyalty to Arthur as the first reason for not acceding to the queen's wishes. This leads to the formality of a trial, which further reveals the inadequacy of the court. The king and the barons are all careful to observe the proper procedure, but the king is also anxious to have a verdict against Lanval in order to satisfy the queen, and some of the barons, although they all seem to be aware of Lanval's innocence, are ready to condemn him just to please the king. Ultimately, the legal system works only because the lady appears, making herself visible to all, and forcing them to see the truth physically. If she had not come, injustice would have prevailed again as it did at the beginning of the story.

The lady's appearance at the court comes after a suspenseful buildup: the arrival of a series of girls, each lovelier than the last, a motif that is probably borrowed from the Tristan stories. It serves both to increase our sense of the lady's beauty and to suggest the way the mind works, beginning with the perception of conventional visible beauty and rising to the concept of ideal beauty. The lady's approach is a slow and stately public progress, in contrast once again to Arthur's anxious attempts to hasten the deliberations of justice. The girls who preceded the lady had all insisted on special preparations, as if Arthur's court were not fit to entertain their mistress, and indeed when she does come she refuses to stay, despite the preparations and the evident desire of all there to serve her. The love she represents cannot be contained in such a world. The hero, who has known the advantages of one and the limitations of the other, makes a total commitment to love: he leaps on her horse as she leaves (from a mounting stone that is used by the heavier men of the court, a sly reminder perhaps of the lightweight nature of most of Arthur's world) and follows her to Avalun, a land that is not of this world.

Les Deus Amanz *(The Two Lovers)*

There happened once in Normandy
a famous adventure
of two young people who loved each other;
both died because of love.
5   The Bretons composed a *lai* about it;
and they gave it the title, *The Two Lovers*.

꙳ The truth is, that in Neustria,
which we call Normandy,
there's a wondrously great, high mountain:
10   the two youngsters lie buried up there.
Near one side of that mountain,
with much deliberation and judgment,
a king who was lord of the Pistrians
had a city built;
15   he named the city after the Pistrians—
he called it Pistre.
The name has lasted ever since;
the town and its dwellings still remain.
We know the region well:
20   it's called the valley of Pistre.
꙳ The king had a beautiful daughter,
an extremely gracious girl.
He found consolation in the maiden
after he had lost his queen.
25   Many reproached him for this—
even his own household blamed him.[1]

---

1. The reason for this attitude on the part of the household is made clearer
by the following lines added after 24 in MSS (S) and (N):

Except for her he had neither son nor daughter;
he cherished her and loved her deeply.
She was wooed by rich men
who would willingly have wed her,
but the king didn't want to give her away

When he heard that people were talking about his conduct
he was saddened and troubled;
he began to consider
30 how he could avoid
anyone's seeking to marry his daughter.
So he sent word far and near, to this effect:
whoever wanted to win his daughter
should know one thing for certain:
35 it was decreed and destined that he
would have to carry her in his arms
to the summit of the mountain outside the city
without stopping to rest.
When the news was known
40 and spread throughout the region,
many attempted the feat,
but couldn't succeed at all.
There were some who pushed themselves so hard
that they carried her halfway up the mountain;
45 yet they couldn't get any farther—
they gave up there.
So, for a long time, he put off giving her away,
because no one wanted to ask for her.
❦ There was a young man in that country,
50 the son of a count, refined and handsome;
he undertook great deeds
to win renown beyond all other men.
He frequented the court of the king—
He stayed there quite often
55 and he came to love the king's daughter,
and many times he pleaded with her
to grant him her love
and become his mistress.
Because he was brave and refined,

---

for he could not do without her.
The king had no other solace;
she was near him night and day.

60 and because the king thought highly of him,
she granted him her love
and he humbly thanked her for it.
They often conversed together
and they loved each other truly,
65 and as much as they could they hid their love
so that no one would discover it.
This restraint disturbed them greatly;
but the young man made up his mind
that he would rather suffer such hardships
70 than be too hasty in his love and thus lose everything.
He was hard pressed by love for her.
So it chanced one day
that the young man—who was so wise, so brave, and so handsome—
came to his beloved
75 and made his complaint to her:
he earnestly begged her
to run away with him—
he couldn't stand the pain any longer;
if he asked her father for her,
80 he knew that the king loved her so much
that he'd refuse to give her up,
unless the suitor could carry her
in his arms to the summit of the mountain.
The maiden answered him:
85 "Dearest," she said, "I know very well
that you couldn't carry me up there for anything:
you aren't strong enough.
If I ran away with you,
my father would be grief-stricken and angry;
90 he would suffer the rest of his life.
Certainly, I love and cherish him enough
that I would never want to upset him.
You'll have to think of another scheme,
because I don't want to hear any more of this one.
95 I have a relative in Salerno,

a rich woman with lots of property;
she's lived there more than thirty years.
She's practiced the medical arts for so long
that she's an expert on medicines.[2]
100 She knows herbs and roots so well
that if you want to go to her
bringing a letter from me with you,
and tell her your problem,
she'll take an interest in it;
105 then she'll make up such prescriptions
and give you such potions
that they'll fortify you,
give you lots of strength.
When you return to this region,
110 you'll ask my father for me;
he'll think you're just a child,
and he'll tell you the agreement—
that he won't give me away to any man,
whatever pains he may take,
115 if he can't carry me up the mountain
in his arms, without stopping to rest."
The youth listened to the idea
and the advice of the maiden;
it delighted him, and he thanked her.
120 He took leave of his mistress,
and went off to his own country.
Quickly he supplied himself
with rich clothes, money,
palfreys and pack mules;
125 only the most trustworthy of his men
did the youth take with him.

---

2. According to many medieval writers, women studied and practiced medicine at Salerno from the eleventh century onward. A gynecological treatise from this period, the *Trotula,* has frequently (but not without objection) been attributed to a Salernitan woman doctor. See A. B. Cobban, *The Medieval Universities* (London, 1975), 40, and works cited in Cobban's notes.

He went to stay in Salerno,
to consult his beloved's aunt.
On her behalf he gave her a letter.
130 When she had read it from one end to the other,
she kept him with her
until she knew all about his situation.
She strengthened him with medicines
and gave him such a potion that,
135 no matter how fatigued he might be,
no matter how constrained, or how burdened,
the potion would still revive his entire body—
even the veins and the bones—
so that he would have all the strength he needed,
140 the moment he drank it.
She poured the potion into a bottle;
he took it back to his own land.³
   The young man, joyful and happy,
wasted no time at home
145 on his return.
He went to the king to ask for his daughter:
if the king would give her to him, he would take her
and carry her to the summit of the mountain.
The king made no attempt to refuse him,
150 though he took him for a great fool,
because the lover was so young.
Many great men, hardy and wise,
had undertaken this task
and none could accomplish it at all!
155 The king named and set a date;
then sent for his vassals, his friends,
everybody he could get;
he wouldn't let anyone stay behind.
Because of his daughter, and the young man
160 who was taking the chance

3. We follow Rychner, who reverses 141 and 142 in MS (H).

of carrying her to the mountain's top,
they came from everywhere.
The damsel prepared herself:
she fasted and dieted,
165   cut down on her eating,
because she desired to help her lover.
⁂ On the day when everyone arrived,
the youth was there first;
he didn't forget to bring his potion.
170   Toward the Seine, out in the meadow,
and into the great crowd assembled there
the king led his daughter.
She wore nothing except her chemise;
her suitor lifted her into his arms.
175   The small phial containing his potion
he gave her to carry in her hand:
he knew well she'd no desire to cheat him.
But I'm afraid the potion did him little good,
because he was entirely lacking in control.
180   Off he went with her at top speed,
and he climbed until he was halfway up the mountain.
In his joy for his beloved
he forgot his potion.
She noticed he was growing weak:
185   "Love," she said, "drink!
I can tell you're getting tired—
now's the time to regain your strength!"
The youth answered:
"Sweetheart, my heart is very strong;
190   I wouldn't stop for any price,
not even long enough to take a drink,
so long as I can still move an inch.
The crowd below would raise a racket,
deafen me with their noise;
195   soon they'd have me all confused.
I don't want to stop here."

When they had gone two thirds of the way up,
he was on the verge of collapsing.
Again and again the maiden begged,
200 "Dearest, take your medicine!"
But he wouldn't listen or take her advice;
in great anguish he staggered on.
He reached the top of the mountain in such pain
that he fell there, and didn't get up;
205 the life went out of his body.
The maiden looked down at her lover,
she thought he had fainted.
She knelt beside him,
attempting to give him his potion;
210 but he couldn't respond to her.
That's how he died, as I've told you.
She grieved for him with loud cries;
she emptied and threw away
the bottle that contained the potion.
215 The mountain got well doused with it,
and the entire region and countryside
were much improved thereby:
many a fine herb now found there
owes its start to the potion.
220 ☙ Now I'll tell you about the damsel:
when she knew she had lost her lover,
you never saw anyone so sad;
she lay down and stretched out beside him,
took him in her arms, pressed him to her,
225 kissed his eyes and lips, again and again;
sorrow for him struck deep in her heart.
She died there too,
that maid who was so brave, so wise, so beautiful.
The king and the others who were waiting for them,
230 when they saw that they weren't returning,
went after them and found them.
The king fell down in a faint.

When he could speak again, he grieved greatly,
and so did all the strangers.
235 They stayed there mourning for three days.
Then they ordered a marble tomb
and placed the two youngsters inside it.
On the advice of everyone present
they buried them on the mountain's summit,
240 and at last they went away.

🌼 Because of the sad adventure of the young folk,
the place is now called the Mount of the Two Lovers.
It happened just the way I've told you;
the Bretons made a *lai* about it.

🌼 LES DEUS AMANZ *(The Two Lovers)*

LES DEUS AMANZ (*The Two Lovers*) takes its name from a
mountain near Pitres, in Normandy, known as the Mont des
Deux Amants, at the top of which remain, to this day, the
ruins of a twelfth-century priory dedicated to "the two lovers."
The lovers thus memorialized were a holy couple, Injuriosus
and Scholastica, who, legend had it, had retired to monastic life
together. Marie borrowed the mountain and its name and
attached to them a fanciful tale of young love thwarted by
parental obstacles and by its own immoderate exuberance.
Les Deus Amanz is also a tissue of literary borrowings from
stories well known to Marie and her audience; by juxtaposing
these often disparate materials—or rather, by crowding them
upon each other within the *lai*'s less than 250 lines—Marie
creates narrative imbalances and uncomfortably sudden shifts
of perspective that undermine the story's potentially serious
impact. Since the *lai* is also full of anticlimax and other comic
manipulations of its characters and situations, there is every
reason to believe that Marie undertook to parody her own art,

and that of other tellers of noble love stories, in *Les Deus Amanz.*

The story of the king who cannot bear to part with his only daughter, and so invents a test that any prospective suitor must pass before marrying her, is a domesticated version of the widely diffused romance of Apollonius of Tyre; in the original, the king's relationship with his daughter is incestuous, and the test, in the form of a riddle, carries with it the death penalty for those who do not solve it. Marie excises both disgust and peril from the story, and thereby trivializes it: the king is a bereaved widower with an understandable, though selfish, desire to retain the consoling presence of his only daughter, and the trial he devises carries with it no penalty for failure save loss of the princess. The ordeal itself is faintly ludicrous: the suitor must carry the princess in his arms to the top of a nearby mountain. Marie proceeds to exploit this situation for comic effect. The young hero of the *lai,* although he is anxious to win surpassing renown by great deeds, is too weak to carry the princess the required distance, as she candidly admits. The impact of this failure of prowess is considerably dulled by the boy's being able to persuade the princess to enter into a secret love relationship with him, thanks to his valor(!), his courtesy, and—most ironic of all—his good standing with the king. After having prudently suffered for a while the inconveniences of such a love, the young man proposes the (unheroic) expedient of elopement, which the princess vetoes on the grounds of her unwillingness to hurt her father. Yet she is quite willing to propose that her lover cheat to pass the ordeal (by means of a strength potion obtained from her aunt in Salerno, a famous medieval center of medical studies), although this ruse proves to hurt her father far more than elopement would have—she dies.

The strength potion is a down-to-earth (and therefore parodistic) version of the love philter or strength-giving magic ring that figures in many medieval romances; a further bathetic touch is the letter of introduction the hero brings with him, on his quest for triumph in love, to Salerno. Meanwhile, as the hour of trial approaches, Marie subverts the heroic enterprise with yet another anticlimactic novelty: the princess undertakes to aid her lover by going on literature's first crash diet. (In fact, if the potion works as planned, the diet will be as unnecessary as it is incongruous.)

Once the young man sets out up the mountain carrying his beloved, Marie's literary model changes from romance to epic—from Apollonius to *The Song of Roland*. Marie signals the change by warning us portentously that the potion won't work because the hero lacks *mesure*—the virtue of moderation inevitably absent from the character of great heroes like Achilles or Roland. The climax of the *lai* comes when the youth, staggering ever more weakly up the mountain, still refuses (for the curious reason that the roar of the crowd of spectators would confuse him if he paused) to drink the potion urged ever more insistently upon him by the princess, who is carrying it for him in a little bottle. The princess's plea, *bevez vostre mescine* ("take your medicine"), echoes Oliver's plea that Roland sound his horn to summon Charles and the Frankish army back to Roncesvalles to save the rearguard; the difference in circumstance defines the distance between heroic intensity and heroic parody. The weight of a fasting princess is neither an expected nor an acceptable instrument of heroic self-confrontation through self-destruction, nor can we suppress the awareness that the princess's exhortations sound uncomfortably like those of a worried mother dosing a sick and cantankerous child.

Having brought her lovers to the summit of their passion, literally and figuratively, Marie has the hero succumb to exhaustion, and, immediately thereafter, the heroine to grief. This bathetic denouement, in which the young lovers are discovered dead by the grieving father (the ultimate cause of their death) and interred in a single tomb, deliberately recalls Ovid's story of Pyramus and Thisbe (*Metamorphoses*, Bk. 4), which was retold as a courtly fable in Marie's day. Marie parodies her "source" by a final, comic metamorphosis when the princess discards the potion; though unused in the cause of love, it proves to be excellent plant food, and causes new, efficacious herbs to grow in the region where it is spilled. (In Ovid's version, Thisbe, before committing suicide over Pyramus's body, prays that the mulberry tree's fruit may become dark red to memorialize the double death; her prayer is granted.) The *lai* ends as it began, in a transparently allusive and euphemistic relationship to literary tradition.

The ostensible message of *Les Deus Amanz* is that love, by inspiring in lovers transcendent joy and daring—the hero forgets the potion in his joy at his beloved—forces them beyond the limits imposed on them by the exigencies of social and familial relationships, and thus destroys them. More persistently, the *lai* urges the fragility of the literary tradition of ennobling, tragic love by hedging the love affair about with details and stratagems that curb its flight toward heroism or even pathos. The potion, intended within the story to bridge the gap between the hero's love aspirations and human limitations, is also a symbol of love's inability to thrive without recourse to trickery and art. The refusal of the potion is at once the triumph and the death of childhood's exalted vision—but the acceptance of the potion would spell the end of the illusion from another point of view. In illustrating the limits of the courtly love vision, Marie demonstrates artistic *démesure*—the use of too many conflicting story models, too tamely retold in too little space—analogous to that of her hero. As a result, the story staggers, as it were, under the weight of its borrowings, and falls repeatedly from the heights of intensity into the valley of anticlimax. Nowhere does Marie show her artistic mastery more clearly than in this joke she plays on herself.

Yonec

Now that I've begun these *lais*
the effort will not stop me;
every adventure that I know
I shall relate in rhyme.
5   My intention and my desire
is to tell you next of Yonec,
how he was born and how his father
first came to his mother.
The man who fathered Yonec
10   was called Muldumarec.

There once lived in Brittany
a rich man, old and ancient.
At Caerwent, he was acknowledged
and accepted as lord of the land.
15   The city sits on the Duelas,
which at one time was open to boats.
The man was very far along in years
but because he possessed a large fortune
he took a wife in order to have children,
20   who would come after him and be his heirs.
The girl who was given to the rich man
came from a good family;
she was wise and gracious[1] and very beautiful—
for her beauty he loved her very much.
25   Because she was beautiful and noble
he made every effort to guard her.
He locked her inside his tower
in a great paved chamber.
A sister of his,
30   who was also old and a widow, without her own lord,
he stationed with his lady
to guard her even more closely.

1. *curteise:* courtly.

There were other women, I believe,
in another chamber by themselves,
35 but the lady never spoke to them
unless the old woman gave her permission.
So he kept her more than seven years—
they never had any children;
she never left that tower,
40 neither for family nor for friends.
When the lord came to sleep there
no chamberlain or porter
dared enter that room,
not even to carry a candle before the lord.
45 The lady lived in great sorrow,
with tears and sighs and weeping;
she lost her beauty,
as one does who cares nothing for it.
She would have preferred
50 death to take her quickly.

It was the beginning of April
when the birds begin their songs.
The lord arose in the morning
and made ready to go to the woods.
55 He had the old woman get up
and close the door behind him—
she followed his command.
The lord went off with his men.
The old woman carried a psalter
60 from which she intended to read the psalms.
The lady, awake and in tears,
saw the light of the sun.
She noticed that the old woman
had left the chamber.
65 She grieved and sighed
and wept and raged:
"I should never have been born!

My fate is very harsh.
I'm imprisoned in this tower
70 and I'll never leave it unless I die.
What is this jealous old man afraid of
that he keeps me so imprisoned?
He's mad, out of his senses;
always afraid of being deceived.
75 I can't even go to church
or hear God's service.
If I could speak to people
and enjoy myself with them
I'd be very gracious to my lord
80 even if I didn't want to be.
A curse on my family,
and on all the others
who gave me to this jealous man,
who married me to his body.
85 It's a rough rope that I pull and draw.
He'll never die—
when he should have been baptized
he was plunged instead in the river of hell;
his sinews are hard, his veins are hard,
90 filled with living blood.
I've often heard
that one could once find
adventures in this land
that brought relief to the unhappy.
95 Knights might find young girls
to their desire, noble and lovely;
and ladies find lovers
so handsome, courtly, brave, and valiant
that they could not be blamed,
100 and no one else would see them.
If that might be or ever was,
if that has ever happened to anyone,
God, who has power over everything,
grant me my wish in this."

105 When she'd finished her lament,
she saw, through a narrow window,
the shadow of a great bird.
She didn't know what it was.
It flew into the chamber;
110 its feet were banded; it looked like a hawk
of five or six moultings.
It alighted before the lady.
When it had been there awhile
and she'd stared hard at it,
115 it became a handsome and noble knight.
The lady was astonished;
her blood went cold, she trembled,
she was frightened—she covered her head.
The knight was very courteous,
120 he spoke first:
"Lady," he said, "don't be afraid.
The hawk is a noble bird,
although its secrets are unknown to you.
Be reassured
125 and accept me as your love.
That," he said, "is why I came here.
I have loved you for a long time,
I've desired you in my heart.
Never have I loved any woman but you
130 nor shall I ever love another,
yet I couldn't have come to you
or left my own land
had you not asked for me.
But now I can be your love."
135 The lady was reassured;
she uncovered her head and spoke.
She answered the knight,
saying she would take him as her lover
if he believed in God,
140 and if their love was really possible.

For he was of great beauty.
Never in her life
had she seen so handsome a knight—
nor would she ever.
145 "My lady," he said, "you are right.
I wouldn't want you to feel
guilt because of me,
or doubt or suspicion.
I do believe in the creator
150 who freed us from the grief
that Adam, our father, led us into
when he bit into the bitter apple.
He is, will be, and always was
the life and light of sinners.
155 If you don't believe me
send for your chaplain.
Say that you've suddenly been taken ill
and that you desire the service
that God established in this world
160 for the healing of sinners.
I shall take on your appearance
to receive the body of our lord God,
and I'll recite my whole credo for you.
You will never doubt my faith again."
165 She answered that she was satisfied.
He lay beside her on the bed
but he didn't try to touch her,
to embrace her or to kiss her.
Meanwhile, the old woman had returned.
170 She found the lady awake
and told her it was time to get up,
she would bring her clothes.
The lady said she was ill,
that the old woman should send for the chaplain
175 and bring him to her quickly—
she very much feared she was dying.

The old woman said, "Be patient,
my lord has gone to the woods.
No one may come in here but me."
180 The lady was very upset;
she pretended to faint.
When the other saw her, she was frightened;
she unlocked the door of the chamber
and sent for the priest.
185 He came as quickly as he could,
bringing the *corpus domini*.[2]
The knight received it,
drank the wine from the chalice.
Then the chaplain left
190 and the old woman closed the doors.
The lady lay beside her love—
there was never a more beautiful couple.
When they had laughed and played
and spoken intimately,
195 the knight took his leave
to return to his land.
She gently begged him
to come back often.
"Lady," he said, "whenever you please,
200 I will be here within the hour.
But you must make certain
that we're not discovered.
This old woman will betray us,
night and day she will spy on us.
205 She will perceive our love,
and tell her lord about it.
If that happens,
if we are betrayed,
I won't be able to escape.
210 I shall die."

2. The body of the Lord, the eucharistic host.

With that the knight departed,
leaving his love in great joy.
In the morning she rose restored;
she was happy all week.
215   Her body had now become precious to her,
she completely recovered her beauty.
Now she would rather remain here
than look for pleasure elsewhere.
She wanted to see her love all the time
220   and enjoy herself with him.
As soon as her lord departed,
night or day, early or late,
she had him all to her pleasure.
God, let their joy endure!
225   Because of the great joy she felt,
because she could see her love so often,
her whole appearance changed.
But her lord was clever.
In his heart he sensed
230   that she was not what she had been.
He suspected his sister.
He questioned her one day,
saying he was astonished
that the lady now dressed with care.
235   He asked her what it meant.
The old woman said she didn't know—
no one could have spoken to her,
she had no lover or friend—
it was only that she was now more willing
240   to be alone than before.
His sister, too, had noticed the change.
Her lord answered:
"By my faith," he said, "I think that's so.
But you must do something for me.
245   In the morning, when I've gotten up
and you have shut the doors,

pretend you are going out
and leave her lying there alone.
Then hide yourself in a safe place,
250 watch her and find out
what it is, and where it comes from,
that gives her such great joy."
With that plan they separated.
Alas, how hard it is to protect yourself
255 from someone who wants to trap you,
to betray and deceive you!

Three days later, as I heard the story,
the lord pretended to go away.
He told his wife the story
260 that the king had sent for him by letter
but that he would return quickly.
He left the chamber and shut the door.
The old woman got up,
went behind a curtain;
265 from there she could hear and see
whatever she wanted to know.
The lady lay in bed but did not sleep,
she longed for her love.
He came without delay,
270 before any time had passed.
They gave each other great joy
with word and look
until it was time to rise—
he had to go.
275 But the old woman watched him,
saw how he came and went.
She was quite frightened
when she saw him first a man and then a bird.
When the lord returned—
280 he hadn't gone very far—
she told him and revealed
the truth about the knight

and the lord was troubled by it.
But he was quick to invent
285 a way to kill the knight.
He had great spikes of iron forged,
their tips sharpened—
no razor on earth could cut better.
When he had them all prepared
290 and pronged on all sides,
he set them in the window—
close together and firmly placed—
through which the knight passed
when he visited the lady.
295 God, he doesn't know what treachery
the villains are preparing.
The next day in the morning
the lord rose before dawn
and said he was going hunting.
300 The old woman saw him to the door
and then went back to bed
for day was not yet visible.
The lady awoke and waited
for the one she loved faithfully;
305 she said he might well come now
and be with her at leisure.
As soon as she asked,
he came without delay.
He flew into the window,
310 but the spikes were there.
One wounded him in his breast—
out rushed the red blood.
He knew he was fatally wounded;
he pulled himself free and entered the room.
315 He alighted on the bed, in front of the lady,
staining the bedclothes with blood.
She saw the blood and the wound
in anguish and horror.
He said, "My sweet love,

320 I lose my life for love of you.
     I told you it would happen,
     that your appearance would kill us."
     When she heard that, she fainted;
     for a short while she lay as if dead.
325 He comforted her gently,
     said that grief would do no good,
     but that she was pregnant with his child.
     She would have a son, brave and strong,
     who would comfort her;
330 she would call him Yonec.
     He would avenge both of them
     and kill their enemy.
     But he could remain no longer
     for his wound was bleeding badly.
335 He left in great sorrow.
     She followed him with loud cries.
     She leapt out a window—
     it's a wonder that she wasn't killed,
     for it was at least twenty feet high
340 where she made her leap,
     naked beneath her gown.
     She followed the traces of blood
     that flowed from the knight
     onto the road.
345 She followed that road and kept to it
     until she came to a hill.
     In the hill there was an opening,
     red with his blood.
     She couldn't see anything beyond it
350 but she was sure
     that her love had gone in there.
     She entered quickly.
     She found no light
     but she kept to the right road
355 until it emerged from the hill

into a beautiful meadow.
When she found the grass there wet with blood,
she was frightened.
She followed the traces through the meadow
360 and saw a city not far away.
The city was completely surrounded by walls.
There was no house, no hall or tower,
that didn't seem entirely of silver.
The buildings were very rich.
365 Going toward the town there were marshes,
forests, and enclosed fields.
On the other side, toward the castle,
a stream flowed all around,
where ships arrived—
370 there were more than three hundred sails.
The lower gate was open;
the lady entered the city,
still following the fresh blood
through the town to the castle.
375 No one spoke to her,
she met neither man nor woman.
When she came to the palace courtyard,
she found it covered with blood.
She entered a lovely chamber
380 where she found a knight sleeping.
She did not know him, so she went on
into another larger chamber.
There she found nothing but a bed
with a knight sleeping on it;
385 she kept going.
She entered the third chamber
and on that bed she found her love.
The feet of the bed were all of polished gold,
I couldn't guess the value of the bedclothes;
390 the candles and the chandeliers,
which were lit night and day,

were worth the gold of an entire city.
As soon as she saw him
she recognized the knight.
395 She approached, frightened,
and fell fainting over him.
He, who greatly loved her, embraced her,
lamenting his misfortune again and again.
When she recovered from her faint
400 he comforted her gently.
"Sweet friend, for God's sake, I beg you,
go away! Leave this place!
I shall die within[3] the day,
there will be great sorrow here,
405 and if you are found
you will be hurt.
Among my people it will be well known
that they have lost me because of my love for you.
I am disturbed and troubled for you."
410 The lady answered: "Love,
I would rather die with you
than suffer with my lord.
If I go back to him he'll kill me."
The knight reassured her,
415 gave her a ring,
and explained to her
that, as long as she kept it,
her lord would not remember
anything that had happened—
420 he would imprison her no longer.
He gave her his sword
and then made her swear
no man would ever possess it,
that she'd keep it for their son.
425 When the son had grown and become

---

3. Rychner, following (P) and (Q), gives *en mi,* "in the middle of the day"; Ewert, with (H) and (S), gives *devant,* "before."

a brave and valiant knight,
she would go to a festival,
taking him and her lord with her.
They would come to an abbey.
430 There, beside a tomb,
they would hear the story of his death,
how he was wrongfully killed.
There she would give her son the sword.
The adventure would be recited to him,
435 how he was born and who his father was;
then they'd see what he would do.
When he'd told her and shown her everything,
he gave her a precious robe
and told her to put it on.
440 Then he sent her away.
She left carrying the ring
and the sword—they comforted her.
She had not gone half a mile
from the gate of the city
445 when she heard the bells ring
and the mourning begin in the castle,
and in her sorrow
she fainted four times.
When she recovered from the faints
450 she made her way to the hill.
She entered it, passed through it,
and returned to her country.
There with her lord
she lived many days and years.
455 He never accused her of that deed,
never insulted or abused her.
Her son was born and nourished,
protected and cherished.
They named him Yonec.
460 In all the kingdom you couldn't find
one so handsome, brave, or strong,
so generous, so munificent.

When he reached the proper age,
he was made a knight.

465 Hear now what happened
in that very year.
To the feast of St. Aaron,
celebrated in Caerleon
and in many other cities,

470 the lord had been summoned
to come with his friends,
according to the custom of the land,
and to bring his wife and his son,
all richly attired.

475 So it was; they went.
But they didn't know the way;
they had a boy with them
who guided them along the right road
until they came to a castle—

480 none more beautiful in all the world.
Inside, there was an abbey
of very religious people.
The boy who was guiding them to the festival
housed them there.

485 In the abbot's chamber
they were well served and honored.
Next day they went to hear Mass
before they departed,
but the abbot went to speak to them

490 to beg them to stay
so he could show them the dormitory,
the chapter house, and the refectory.
And since they were comfortable there,
the lord agreed to stay.

495 That day, after they had dined,
they went to the workshops.
On their way, they passed the chapter house,
where they found a huge tomb
covered with a cloth of embroidered silk,

500 a band of precious gold running from one side to the other.
     At the head, the feet, and at the sides
     burned twenty candles.
     The chandeliers were pure gold,
     the censers amethyst,
505 which through the day perfumed
     that tomb, to its great honor.
     They asked and inquired
     of people from that land
     whose tomb it was,
510 what man lay there.
     The people began to weep
     and, weeping, to recount
     that it was the best knight
     the strongest, the most fierce,
515 the most handsome and the best loved,
     that had ever lived.
     "He was king of this land;
     no one was ever so courtly.
     At Caerwent he was discovered
520 and killed for the love of a lady.
     Since then we have had no lord,
     but have waited many days,
     just as he told and commanded us,
     for the son the lady bore him."
525 When the lady heard that news,
     she called aloud to her son.
     "Fair son," she said, "you hear
     how God has led us to this spot.
     Your father, whom this old man murdered,
530 lies here in this tomb.
     Now I give and commend his sword to you.
     I have kept it a long time for you."
     Then she revealed, for all to hear,
     that the man in the tomb was the father and this was his son,
535 and how he used to come to her,
     how her lord had betrayed him—

she told the truth.
Then she fainted over the tomb
and, in her faint, she died.
540 She never spoke again.
When her son saw that she had died,
he cut off his stepfather's head.
Thus with his father's sword
he avenged his mother's sorrow.
545 When all this had happened,
when it became known through the city,
they took the lady with great honor
and placed her in the coffin.
Before they departed
550 they made Yonec their lord.

Long after, those who heard this adventure
composed a lay about it,
about the pain and the grief
that they suffered for love.

YONEC

YONEC begins with what appears to be a conventional literary
situation, an old and jealous husband keeping his young wife
under close guard. The audience expects a plot to deceive the
husband and smuggle in a young lover. A young lover does
indeed make his way to the wife, but otherwise, in all the
details and in the overall tone of the story, the treatment is
quite unusual. The lovers do not use their wits to deceive the
husband—it is the husband who plots to trap and kill the lover,
while the wife uses her imagination to create the kind of love
she needs.

The wife is young and lovely, with all the social graces, but
these are wasted in the tower in which she is imprisoned; the

husband, wanting to keep her charms all to himself, only des-
troys them. He is too old, a point underlined in the French
by the repetition of the word *trespas* (l. 16) in *trespassez*
(l. 17): the river of his city once offered a *trespas,* "passage,"
to boats, that is, it has since dried up; and the husband is
mult trespassez, "very far along in years," presumably also
dried up. Furthermore, his love is possessive, life-denying—
he married supposedly to have heirs, but the marriage is child-
less—and ultimately evil. He will not allow his wife even to go
to church and she accuses her family of committing a grave
sin in marrying her to this man; she suspects that he was
baptized in the waters of hell. As if to emphasize the husband's
evil, the lover's first act when he comes to the lady is to ask
for a priest and take the host.

The love, in other words, is not a sin. In fact, it restores the
lady's beauty and joy (joy is the dominant theme in the love
scenes, the word *joie* is constantly repeated), so that even the
husband notices the change. That is what drives him to search
out and destroy the lover who is the source of it. The husband
is a hunter—he is always leaving to go off to the forest—and
he sets a particularly vicious trap for his prey, the lover who
comes to the lady in the shape of a bird. The bird, a hawk,
is at once the only creature who could gain entrance to the
tower and a symbol of the lover in lyric poetry. He is also, by
nature, a predator, a hunter, but the bird-knight of this story, in
another reversal of expectation, is a gentle, tame creature who
comes at the lady's call to bring her love and joy.

The lady, forced inward on herself by the lack of love in her
marriage and the absence of family or friends to console her,
escapes into her imagination. She thinks of adventures, which
she associates with blameless love between knights and ladies;
she prays for one to come to her, and the bird appears. As she
stares at it, it becomes a handsome man. That is, her will brings
him, and her look gives him form. But when the reality of
her world intrudes on her fantasy, when the husband discovers
the existence of the bird, the dream is shattered, destroyed by
his envy. The bird, wounded by the husband's trap, withdraws

forever. But love has given the lady the power to overcome the problems of her life. She is able to leave her prison (she leaps from a window of the tower without injury), follow her dying lover to his land, and then return to her husband, but she is never again to be imprisoned by him.

The lover's land is a kind of dream world, a city of silver that she reaches by making her way through a long, dark tunnel. When she enters his palace, she goes through room after room of sleeping knights. Her own life is in danger here, as her lover's was in her husband's tower; when her dream is taken from her, she loses the desire to live. But her lover tells her that she will have a son and gives her a sword to keep for him, so that he can one day avenge them and their love. It is the child who gives reality to the love; it is through him that the love can endure.

What Marie seems to be saying in this *lai,* as in several others, is that the world can imprison the body but not the mind, once the mind wills itself free. Love gives the lady the power, by giving her the will, to free herself.

Laustic (*The Nightingale*)

I shall tell you an adventure
about which the Bretons made a *lai*.
Laüstic was the name, I think,
they gave it in their land.
5   In French it is *rossignol,*
and *nightingale* in proper English.
At Saint-Malo, in that country,
there was a famous city.
Two knights lived there,
10   they both had strong houses.
From the goodness of the two barons
the city acquired a good name.
One had married a woman
wise, courtly, and handsome;
15   she set a wonderfully high value on herself,
within the bounds of custom and usage.
The other was a bachelor,
well known among his peers
for bravery and great valor;
20   he delighted in living well.
He jousted often, spent widely
and gave out what he had.
He also loved his neighbor's wife;
he asked her, begged her so persistently,
25   and there was such good in him,
that she loved him more than anything,
as much for the good that she heard of him
as because he was close by.
They loved each other discreetly and well,
30   concealed themselves and took care
that they weren't seen
or disturbed or suspected.
And they could do this well enough
since their dwellings were close,

155

35 their houses were next door,
and so were their rooms and their towers;
there was no barrier or boundary
except a high wall of dark stone.
From the rooms where the lady slept,
40 if she went to the window
she could talk to her love
on the other side, and he to her,
and they could exchange their possessions,
by tossing and throwing them.
45 There was scarcely anything to disturb them,
they were both quite at ease;
except that they couldn't come together
completely for their pleasure,
for the lady was closely guarded
50 when her husband was in the country.
Yet they always managed,
whether at night or in the day,
to be able to talk together;
no one could prevent
55 their coming to the window
and seeing each other there.
For a long time they loved each other,
until one summer
when the woods and meadows were green
60 and the orchards blooming.
The little birds, with great sweetness,
were voicing their joy above the flowers.
It is no wonder if he understands them,
he who has love to his desire.
65 I'll tell you the truth about the knight:
he listened to them intently
and to the lady on the other side,
both with words and looks.
At night, when the moon shone
70 when her lord was in bed,

she often rose from his side
and wrapped herself in a cloak.
She went to the window
because of her lover, who, she knew,
75 was leading the same life,
awake most of the night.
Each took pleasure in the other's sight
since they could have nothing more;
but she got up and stood there so often
80 that her lord grew angry
and began to question her, to ask
why she got up and where she went.
"My lord," the lady answered him,
"there is no joy in this world
85 like hearing the nightingale sing.
That's why I stand there.
It sounds so sweet at night
that it gives me great pleasure;
it delights me so and I so desire it
90 that I cannot close my eyes."
When her lord heard what she said
he laughed in anger and ill will.
He set his mind on one thing:
to trap the nightingale.
95 There was no valet in his house
that he didn't set to making traps, nets, or snares,
which he then had placed in the orchard;
there was no hazel tree or chestnut
where they did not place a snare or lime
100 until they trapped and captured him.
When they had caught the nightingale,
they brought it, still alive, to the lord.
He was very happy when he had it;
he came to the lady's chambers.
105 "Lady," he said, "where are you?
Come here! Speak to us!

I have trappèd the nightingale
that kept you awake so much.
From now on you can lie in peace:
110   he will never again awaken you."
When the lady heard him,
she was sad and angry.
She asked her lord for the bird
but he killed it out of spite,
115   he broke its neck in his hands—
too vicious an act—
and threw the body on the lady;
her shift was stained with blood,
a little, on her breast.
120   Then he left the room.
The lady took the little body;
she wept hard and cursed
those who betrayed the nightingale,
who made the traps and snares,
125   for they took great joy from her.
"Alas," she said, "now I must suffer.
I won't be able to get up at night
or go and stand in the window
where I used to see my love.
130   I know one thing for certain:
he'd think I was pretending.
I must decide what to do about this.
I shall send him the nightingale
and relate the adventure."
135   In a piece of samite,
embroidered in gold and writing,
she wrapped the little bird.
She called one of her servants,
charged him with her message,
140   and sent him to her love.
He came to the knight,
greeted him in the name of the lady,

related the whole message to him,
and presented the nightingale.

145 When everything had been told and revealed to the knight,
after he had listened well,
he was very sad about the adventure,
but he wasn't mean or hesitant.
He had a small vessel fashioned,
150 with no iron or steel in it;
it was all pure gold and good stones,
very precious and very dear;
the cover was very carefully attached.
He placed the nightingale inside
155 and then he had the casket sealed—
he carried it with him always.

This adventure was told,
it could not be concealed for long.
The Bretons made a *lai* about it
160 which men call *The Nightingale*.

🦋 L A Ü S T I C *(The Nightingale)*

LAÜSTIC offers us an unusual variation on the idea of art as the preserver or embodier of love. In this *lai*, the dead bird in the jeweled casket is the symbol of a love that had little substance to begin with. The love has no apparent reason for beginning or continuing, except for the amusement of the two lovers. The lady accepts the man's love as much because he is her next-door neighbor as because he has a good reputation. Their physical proximity makes it easy for them to talk and even to toss gifts back and forth, despite the husband's close guarding of his wife. At the same time, the lovers are confined by the very walls that bring them together.[1] The lady can look out from her room into another life, but she is not able to enter it. Since, in other *lais,* the will to go is enough (*Guigemar, Yonec, Lanval*), we must assume that her love lacks force. It ends symbolically confined in an even smaller space, the casket.

The love that is carried on over or through a wall separating two houses is, of course, reminiscent of the Pyramis and Thisbe story, but Marie has changed the innocent affection of two children to a self-indulgent flirtation between two adults, the man a friend of the woman's husband. The lovers indulge themselves like children: the lady gets up so often in the middle of the night to speak with her lover that her husband becomes suspicious. Marie seems to feel little sympathy for this love—for the man it means the betrayal of a friend; for the woman, the deceiving of a husband. The phrase "he also loved his neighbor's wife" (l. 23) suggests a moral criticism as well.

Disapproval of the lovers does not mean that we are to take the husband's part. His reaction to his wife's story about the nightingale is so cruel, so gratuitously vicious, that even though his victim is a bird and not the lover (in contrast to *Yonec*),[2] we are shocked. Marie tells us that one who loves understands the songs of the bird, so when the husband kills the bird, we infer how impossible it is for him to understand love. His actions are so exaggerated in view of the aim—traps are made and set in every tree in order to capture one small bird, the bird is murdered in front of the wife and the bloody body tossed on her breast—that we can only be horrified and disgusted. And yet the effect on his wife is much slighter than we might have expected: only a little blood stains her shift; she weeps and curses but she accepts the situation very quickly. No plots are devised, no new ways to communicate are sought. Both lovers give up quite easily.

This is a very different ending from the analogous story about the poet Guilhem de Cabestaing as it is told in his *vida;* there the lover is killed in an ambush by the lady's husband, who feeds the lover's heart to his wife. When he tells her what it was, she vows never to eat any other food and throws herself from the balcony.[3] Although this version is later than Marie's, there are similar folktales which Marie might well have known. In any case, the difference in her version shows that she is not concerned here with a tragic tale of passion but with a short-lived, self-indulgent affair. At the end of her *lai,* all that remains of the love is the bird that lies with his neck broken in a splendid coffin of gold and jewels, an artifact which, like the love, displays all its wealth on the surface. Because it is a self-indulgent love, it cannot bear fruit. The bird symbol cannot be replaced by or live on in a son, as in *Yonec* and *Milun;* it can only die.

Since the nightingale is also a symbol of the poet, the singer of love songs, Marie may be saying that art, too, preserves dead events in an elaborate setting. This rather negative view of her art, not unusual in medieval literature, is unusual for Marie, but we will find it again in *Chaitivel.* Presumably, if the subject of the art, in this case the love, has no substance, the art that re-creates it can be only an empty shell.

1. R. D. Cottrell suggests that Marie concentrates on the area of drama by progressively delimiting the geographical confines. "As the spatial dimension of the story contracts, the lovers' frustration increases" (" 'Le Lai du Laüstic': From Physicality to Spirituality," *Philological Quarterly* 47 (1968), 502.

2. J. Ribard points out that the lover is a shadowy figure until the end of the *lai,* that he is almost a figment of the imagination like the bird-knight in *Yonec,* but he does not materialize ("Le lai du Laostic: Structure et significa-tion," *Le Moyen Age* 76 [1970], 269).

3. Boccaccio tells the same story in the *Decameron,* IV, 9. It is also told in the twelfth-century poem *The Owl and the Nightingale;* the owl tells how the husband catches his nightingale and draws and quarters it (ll. 1049–62) and later the nightingale tells how the husband was punished (ll. 1075–1110). There are other versions in which the death of the nightingale leads the lover to kill the husband and marry the lady.

Milun

🙰 Whoever wants to tell a variety of stories
ought to have a variety of beginnings,
and speak so intelligently
that people will enjoy listening.
5 Now I'll begin *Milun*
and show, in a brief discourse,
why and how the *lai*
called by that name was written.[1]
🙰 Milun was born in South Wales.
10 From the day he was dubbed knight
he couldn't find a single opponent
who could knock him off his horse.
He certainly was a good knight:
generous and strong, courteous and proud.
15 He won fame in Ireland,
in Norway and Gothland;
in Logres and in Albany
many envied him.
He was well beloved
20 and honored by many princes.
🙰 There was a baron in his country—
I don't know his name—
who had a daughter,
a beautiful and most refined girl.
25 She had heard of Milun,
and began to love him.
She sent a messenger to him,
to say that, if it pleased him, she would love him.
Milun was happy with the news,
30 and thanked the girl;
he willingly granted her his love,
and said he would never leave her;

---

1. The French term, *trovez,* could also be rendered "composed," if Marie
is referring to a musical setting.

his response to her was very courtly,
and he gave rich gifts to the messenger,
35 promising him his friendship.
"My friend," he said, "please undertake
to help me speak to my beloved
and to keep our communications secret.
Carry my gold ring to her
40 and tell her on my behalf:
whenever she wants, she can send you for me
and I'll go with you."
The messenger took his leave and soon went away;
he returned to his lady.
45 He gave her the ring and told her
that he had done what she had asked.
The girl was delighted
at the love she was being offered.
Outside her room, in a grove
50 where she went to amuse herself,
she and Milun, very often,
had a rendezvous.
Milun came there so often and loved her so much
that the girl became pregnant.
55 When she realized this,
she sent for Milun and made her lament.
She told him what had happened;
she had lost her honor and her good name
when she got herself into this situation.
60 She would be grievously punished:
tortured by the sword
or sold into slavery in another land.
Such were the ancient customs
observed in those days.
65 Milun answered that he would do
whatever she counseled.
"When the child is born," she said,
"you must bring him to my sister,
who is married and living in Northumbria;

70 she is a rich woman, worthy and prudent.
    And send word to her, in writing
    and also orally
    that this child belongs to her sister,
    who has endured great grief because of him.
75 She should make sure that he's well nourished,
    whatever it may be, son or daughter.
    I shall hang your ring around his neck
    and send a letter with it,
    in which will be written his father's name
80 and the unfortunate story of his mother.[2]
    When he is full grown,
    and has arrived at the age
    when he can listen to reason,
    she should give him the ring and the letter
85 and command him to keep them
    so that he can find his father."
       They abided by this plan,
    and the time eventually came
    for the girl to have her baby.
90 An old woman who watched over her,
    to whom she had disclosed her entire situation,
    covered things up so well
    that she was never discovered,
    by her words or appearance.
95 The girl had a beautiful son.
    They hung the ring around his neck,
    and also a silken wallet
    with the letter in it, so that no one could see it.
    Then they laid the child in a little cradle,
100 wrapped in a white linen cloth;
    beneath his head
    they placed a fine pillow
    and over him a coverlet,
    hemmed all around with marten fur.

---

2. Once again, Marie uses the key term *aventure*.

105 The old nurse gave him to Milun,
    who was waiting for her in the grove.
    He turned the child over to some trustworthy retainers
    who would take him to his destination.
    As they traveled from town to town,
110 they stopped to rest seven times a day;
    they had the child nursed,
    changed, and bathed.
    They took their job so seriously
    that they had brought a wet nurse with them.[3]
115 They stayed on the right road
    until they reached the sister and gave the child to her.
    She took him from them, and was very pleased with him.
    She also took the letter with its seal.
    When she knew who he was,
120 she cherished him even more.
    Then the men who had brought the child
    returned to their own land.
    Milun left his homeland
    to seek honor through martial exploits.[4]
125 His mistress remained at home
    and her father gave her in marriage
    to a rich lord of the region,
    a powerful man of great repute.
    When she found out about this turn of events,[5]
130 she was grief-stricken,
    and she cried for Milun.
    She was especially worried about being blamed
    for having had a child already;
    her husband would discover that soon enough.
135 "Alas," she said, "what can I do?
    Must I be married? How can I?
    I'm no longer a virgin,

3. Lines 113–114 are omitted by Rychner and Warnke from their editions.
4. The text uses the term *sudees*, meaning paid military service. Cf. the endnote to *Guigemar*, note 2.
5. French: *aventure*.

I'll have to be a servant all my life.
I didn't know it would be like this;
140 rather, I thought I could have my love,
that we could keep it a secret between us,
that I'd never hear it bruited about.
Now I'd rather die than live,
but I'm not even free to do that,
145 since I have guardians all around me,
old and young; my chamberlains,
who hate a noble love,
and take their delight in sadness.
Now I have to suffer like this—
150 if only I could die!"
The time came for her to be married,
and her father led her to the altar.
Milun came back to his land;
he was sad and upset—
155 he gave himself up to grief.
He took some comfort from the fact
that the one he loved so much
was still in her country, nearby.
Milun undertook to plan
160 how he could send word to her—
without being discovered—
that he had come home.
He wrote a letter and sealed it.
He had a swan of which he was very fond;
165 he tied the letter to its neck,
hid it among the feathers.
He summoned one of his squires
and made him his messenger.
"Go immediately and change your clothes," he said.
170 "I want you to go to my mistress' castle,
and take my swan with you.
Make arrangements
for the swan to be given to her
by a servant or a maid."

175 The squire did his duty.
He went off quickly, taking the swan with him;
by the most direct route he knew
he came to the castle.
He went through the village
180 directly to the main gate,
called out to the porter:
"Friend," he said, "listen!
This is how I make a living:
I go around catching birds.
185 In a meadow outside Caerleon
I captured a swan in my net.
To earn her goodwill and support,
I want to make a present of it to the lady of the castle,
so that I won't be bothered
190 while I'm working in this area."
The porter replied,
"Friend, no one can speak to her;
but nonetheless, I'll go find out:
if I can find a place
195 that I can bring you to,
I'll arrange for you to speak with her."
❧ The porter went to the main hall
and found only two knights there,
seated at a big table
200 amusing themselves at chess.
Quickly he returned to the messenger,
and brought him in in such a way
that he wasn't seen
or disturbed by anyone.
205 He came to the lady's chamber, and called;
a girl opened the door for them.
They came into the lady's presence,
presented her with the swan.
She called one of her valets
210 and said to him, "Make it your business
to take good care of my swan;

be sure he has enough food."
"My lady," said the messenger who brought the swan,
"No one but you should have him;
215 this is indeed a royal present—
see how fine and handsome a bird he is!"
He placed the bird in her hands.
She accepted it quite willingly,
petted its neck and head,
220 and felt the letter among the feathers.
Her blood ran cold; she shivered,
realizing the letter was from her lover.
She had some money given to the messenger,
and told him to go.
225 ℣ When the chamber was empty
she called one of her maids.
She detached the letter,
broke the seal.
She read at the top of the sheet, "Milun,"
230 and when she saw her lover's name
she kissed it a hundred times, crying,
before she could read further.
At the beginning of the letter she read
what he had written
235 of the great sadness
from which he was suffering night and day.
Now it was entirely in her power
to kill or cure him.
If she could think of a scheme
240 whereby he could speak with her,
she should let him know in a letter
and send the swan back to him.
First she should have the swan well guarded,
then keep him fasting
245 three days without any food.
Then the letter should be hung on his neck,
and he should be released; he would fly

to where he had formerly lived.
When she had looked at the whole letter,
250 and heard the contents,
she had the swan well taken care of
with abundant food and drink;
she kept him in her chamber for a month.
Now listen to what happened!
255 She used her ingenuity so well
that she obtained some ink and parchment;
she wrote the letter she wanted to,
and sealed it with a ring.
Then she made the swan go hungry,
260 hung the letter on his neck, released him.
The bird was famished—
he really wanted food;
so he quickly returned
to where he had come from—
265 the same town, the same household—
there he landed at Milun's feet.
When Milun saw him, he was very joyful;
he quickly grabbed him by the wings,
he called his steward,
270 had him give the swan some food,
and meanwhile took the letter from his neck.
He read it from one end to the other,
noting all the words that he found in it,
and rejoicing at her message:
275 "She couldn't have any pleasure without him,
and now he should send back his feelings to her,
by the swan, the same way she had done."
He'll do that right away!
For twenty years they lived like this,
280 Milun and his mistress.
The swan was their messenger,
they had no other means of communication,
and they always made him fast
before they let him go on his errand;

285 whoever the bird came to,
     you can be sure, fed it well.
        They met together several times.
     (No one can be so constrained
     or so closely guarded
290 that he can't find a way out.)
        Meanwhile, the lady who had raised their son
     had him dubbed a knight;
     he had been with her long enough
     to come of age.
295 He had become a fine young man.
     She gave him the letter and the ring,
     told him who his mother was,
     and his father's story as well:
     how his father was a good knight,
300 so bold, hardy, and proud
     that there was none who exceeded him
     in worth or valor anywhere.
     When the lady had told him all this
     and he'd listened carefully to her,
305 he rejoiced in his father's virtues;
     he was delighted with what he had learned.
     He said to himself,
     "A man oughtn't to think he's worth much,
     being born in such a manner
'310 and having such a famous father,
     if he doesn't seek out even greater renown
     away from home, in foreign lands."
     He had everything he needed;
     he didn't stay beyond that night,
315 but took his leave next morning.
     His foster mother admonished him,
     urging him to do good deeds;
     she also gave him plenty of money.
        He went to Southampton to get under way;
320 as quickly as he could he set out to sea.

He arrived at Barfleur
and went right to Brittany.
There he spent lavishly and tourneyed,
and became acquainted with rich men.
325 In every joust he entered,
he was judged the best combatant.
He loved poor knights;
what he gained from rich ones
he gave to them and thus retained them in his service;
330 he was generous in all his spending.
He would never willingly stay long in one place;
in all those foreign lands
he won renown for his heroic virtues.
He also excelled in refined and honorable behavior.
335 Because of his excellence and fame
the news spread to his own country
that a young knight of that land,
who had gone abroad to seek honor,
had so excelled in prowess,
340 goodness, and generosity
that those who didn't know his name
called him, everywhere, "the knight without equal."
Milun heard this stranger praised
and his virtues recounted.
345 He was saddened, and complained to himself
about this knight who was worth so much
that, so long as he traveled,
fought in tournaments, and bore arms,
no one else born in that land
350 would be praised or honored.
Milun came to a decision:
he would quickly cross the sea
and joust with this knight,
in order to do some harm to him and his reputation.
355 Anger spurred him on
to try to unhorse the knight—

that would put him to shame!
Then he would go look for his son
who had left the country;
360 Milun did not know what had become of him.
    He let his mistress know his scheme,
and asked her leave to go;
he revealed his intentions
by sending her a sealed letter,
365 by the swan, I believe;
now she had to let him know how she felt.
When she heard his wish,
she thanked him, expressing her gratitude
that he wanted to leave the country
370 to find their son,
and to find out about his fortunes;
she wouldn't interfere with his plans.
Milun got her message,
then dressed himself richly
375 and went over to Normandy,
whence he traveled to Brittany.
He made many acquaintances,
sought out many tournaments;
his lodgings were usually luxurious,
380 and he gave suitably generous gifts.
    Through an entire winter, I believe,
Milun stayed in that land.
He obtained the services of many good knights,
until Easter came,
385 when tournaments began again,
as well as wars and other battles.[6]
A tournament was held at Mont Saint Michel;
Normans and Bretons,
Flemings and Frenchmen all came,

6. During much of the Middle Ages, the times of year when the Church permitted warfare and tournaments were strictly limited, by the concept of the "truce of God." Lent, the period of penance before Easter, was one such time of truce. (The Church's ban was not always observed.)

390 though there were few English knights.
    Milun came early,
    good knight that he was.
    He inquired after the knight without equal;
    there were plenty of knights who could tell him
395 where he had come from.
    By his arms and shield
    he was pointed out to Milun,
    who observed him carefully.
    The tournament began.
400 Whoever wanted to joust quickly found the opportunity;
    he need only search the ranks a bit
    to find a companion
    in the quest for victory or defeat.
    This much I'll tell you about Milun:
405 it went very well with him in combat
    and he was highly praised that day.
    But the young man of whom I've told you—
    he was acclaimed beyond all others;
    none could equal him
410 in tourneying and jousting.
    Milun watched him perform,
    riding and attacking so well;
    although he was Milun's rival,
    he pleased Milun greatly.
415 Milun rushed into the ranks against him,
    and the two jousted together.
    Milun struck him so hard
    that his lance splintered,
    but he didn't unhorse him.
420 The other knight struck Milun so hard
    that he knocked him right off his steed.
    Beneath Milun's visor,
    he saw his beard and white hair;
    he was sorry to have made him fall.
425 He took Milun's horse by the reins,
    and presented it to him,

saying, "My lord, remount;
I'm saddened
that I should have so humiliated
430 a man of your age."
Milun leaped up, highly pleased,
for he had recognized the ring on the other's finger
when he gave Milun his horse.
He spoke to the young man.
435 "My friend," he said, "listen to me!
For the love of almighty God
tell me your father's name!
What is yours? Who is your mother?
I want to know the truth about this.
440 I've seen a lot, wandered a lot,
searched in many lands
in tournaments and wars;
I never once fell from my war-horse
because of a blow from another knight.
445 You knocked me down in a joust—
I could love you a great deal."
The other answered, "I'll tell you
about my father, as much as I know of him.
I think he was born in Wales
450 and is named Milun.
He loved the daughter of a rich man
and secretly conceived me with her.
I was sent to Northumbria,
and there I was raised and educated
455 by my aunt.
She kept me with her,
then gave me a horse and my arms,
and sent me to this land,
where I have long resided.
460 It is my desire and intent
to go back across the sea quickly
and return to my own land;

I wish to find out who my father is,
and how he is behaving toward my mother.
465 I'll show him my gold ring
and tell him my story;
he will certainly not reject me,
rather, as a loving father he'll make much of me."
When Milun heard him say all this
470 he didn't wait to hear any more;
he quickly leapt forward
and took the other by the skirt of his hauberk.
"God!" he cried, "I'm a new man!
By my faith, friend, you are my son!
475 It was to look for you
that I left my homeland this year."
When the young knight heard him, he got down from his horse
and kissed his father warmly.
They both looked so happy
480 and said such things to each other
that all the others watching them
began to cry from joy and pity.
✿ When the tournament broke up,
Milun went away, very anxious
485 to speak at leisure with his son,
to find out what his pleasure was.
They spent the night in a hostel
where there was much celebrating
being done by a large number of knights.
490 Milun told his son
how he loved the boy's mother,
and how her father had given her
to a baron of that region,
and how he had continued loving her,
495 and she him, with all her heart,
and how he used the swan as a messenger,
having the bird carry his letters,
since he couldn't trust anyone else.
The son responded, "Indeed, my good father,

500 I'll bring you and my mother together;
I shall kill her husband
and see you married."
    They spoke no more about it;
the next day they made ready to leave.
505 They said good-bye to their friends,
and returned to their own land.
Their crossing was speedy,
thanks to a good strong wind.
As they went on their way
510 they met a boy
coming from Milun's mistress;
he was on his way to Brittany,
for she had dispatched him to go there.
Now his trip was shortened.
515 She was sending Milun a sealed letter
with a message telling him
that he should come to her without delay:
her husband was dead—now was the time to make haste!
Milun heard the news,
520 and it seemed wonderful to him.
Then he told his son.
Nothing held them back now;
they pushed on until they came
to the lady's castle.
525 She was delighted with her son,
who was so worthy and well behaved.
Without consulting any relatives,
with no advice from anyone else,
their son brought them together,
530 gave his mother to his father.
In great happiness and well-being
they lived happily ever after.

    The ancients made a *lai*
about their love and good fortune;

535 and I who have put it down in writing
have thoroughly enjoyed retelling it.

❧ MILUN

MILUN is one of Marie's more precisely localized *lais*. The hero
and heroine come from South Wales;[1] the child of their love
match is sent to be raised by an aunt in Northumbria; Milun—
and later his son—goes to Brittany by way of Southampton,
seeking *pris,* the honor that comes from the successful exercise
of prowess in chivalric combat. Within this circumstantial
setting, Marie develops a story of chivalry, love, and a family
divided and reconciled. *Milun* resembles *Yonec* in many
particulars, but its characters and situations are treated in a
strikingly different fashion.

One of the peculiarities of *Milun* is its central concern with
communication. The relationship between Milun and his mis-
tress is sustained for twenty years by means of a swan that flies
back and forth with a message hidden beneath its feathers. The
other important means of communication is the gold ring that
Milun sends to his mistress (when she first seeks his love) as a
sign that he will come to her whenever she wishes. The ring
functions as a symbol of the fulfilled relationship; it is used to
set up meetings that lead to the girl's pregnancy, and when her
son is born and sent north, it goes with him, to be given him
(along with a letter revealing his parents' identity) when he
comes of age. Eventually, the ring will reveal the son to his
father during the tournament where they meet and fight each
other.

The climactic encounter between son and father has clear
implications for the view of chivalry and love advanced by the
lai. Milun and his son are the best knights of their respective

generations; neither is ever unhorsed in combat until the younger so humbles the father in the joust just mentioned. The "law" of chivalry, with its relentless quest to gain and maintain *pris,* forces each new generation into combat with the one before. In its pure form, such chivalry takes no heed of other forms of relationship that might modify or cancel its sole criterion of categorization: winners and losers. Though Milun admires the young "knight without equal" when he observes him at a tournament, his pleasure is mingled with resentment that the other is threatening his preeminence among knights; accordingly, he must challenge him, and so the son comes to defeat his father—a moment of potential pathos and outrage recalling the ousting, in Greek mythology, of the ruler of the gods by the hero of the next generation of Olympians (Uranus by Cronos, Cronos by Zeus). The armored knight sees in other knights only foes; the battle between Milun and his son shows how total commitment to prowess and *pris* blinds one to crucial differences of individual identity in others, while obscuring one's own identity as well.[2]

When he sees his rival's white hair, Milun's son—who is, we have been told, of noble character—regrets his deed of violence and holds out to the fallen knight the reins of his horse. By this anticompetitive gesture of compassion, the son reveals the ring and his identity to his father. Discovery of kinship halts a rivalry that would never have taken place had not the two men put the quest of honor above all else in their lives. Marie indicates this dubious set of priorities by telling us that the son, upon learning who his father is, sets out, not to find his parents, but to win fame greater than his father's, i.e., to compete with the preceding generation (as will literally happen when he meets Milun) instead of being united to it by ties of love. When Milun, on the other hand, hears of this (unrecognized) knight's prowess in Brittany, he grieves that there is now a better knight than he, and sets out to challenge him, *after* which he will seek his missing son. (The son mentions his intent to seek his parents only in telling Milun his life history after their joust.) Only the ring prevents patricidal tragedy and brings about the reunion the two knights have delayed in seeking. Love, with its legacy from one generation to the next (symbolized by the ring), neutralizes the dangerous legacy of chivalric *pris*.

Until this climactic moment, love is not a strong enough force in the *lai* to counter either Milun's prowess impulse or his mistress' social bondage. The lovers meet in secret, and make no attempt to marry or run away when their son is conceived; they never defy the social forces threatening or hindering their love. Instead, they send their son away, further sundering the love unit. Then, in a gesture that both symbolizes their separation and contrasts Milun's boldness in chivalry with his furtiveness in love, he leaves his mistress and seeks *pris* once again.[3] While Milun is away, his mistress is forced into a loveless and dangerous marriage—dangerous because her husband may discover she is not a virgin. Milun returns to find even greater obstacles than before to seeing and communicating with his beloved, and solves them ingeniously by using the swan as a messenger. During their twenty-year (!) dependence on the swan, they also meet several times, despite the close surveillance over the wife.[4] This seems small reward for their love; in fact, the starved swan, bringing messages to and from the love-starved pair, becomes a symbol of their undernourished relationship that survives on words alone because of Milun's passivity.

Only at the end of the *lai* does the son, after his reunion with Milun, suggest an active response to the forces that have splintered the love unit: he will do what his father has not done— kill the husband and arrange his parents' marriage. His resolution and vigor imply Marie's criticism of Milun's dilatoriness in his own cause. The message that the two knights receive on their way to South Wales—the husband is dead; Milun should return at once—serves Marie not simply as a device to avoid unpleasant bloodshed and a reliance on the same denouement as *Yonec*'s, but as a way of suggesting that as soon as love begins to control prowess, directing its energies to bind together rather than to separate the love unit, the apparently insuperable social obstacles to love's fulfillment simply disappear.

Milun, then, is an anti-*Yonec* (as *Equitan* is an anti-*Guigemar*), in which the father-lover remains alive and the husband dies conveniently instead of being killed by a vengeful stepson. Neither *lai,* of course, expresses Marie's last word on the subject; each responds to an imaginative view about the power and fruitfulness of love in a world dominated by other value systems—in *Milun,* especially chivalry—that exert centrifugal force on the love relationship.

1. It has been argued that the lovers' use of a swan is a realistic touch since swans breed in certain parts of South Wales.

2. The limitations of a life dedicated to prowess are similarly explored in twelfth-century chivalric romances by Chrétien de Troyes and Hue de Roteland, among others.

3. The emphasis on Milun's inseparability from his horse in battle at the beginning of the *lai* is perhaps intended as a contrast to the easy separability of Milun from his mistress; the parallel would derive force from the literary convention of referring to sexual relations under the metaphor of horse riding, as in a troubadour lyric of Guillaume IX, and possibly the protagonist's name in *Equitan.*

4. Marie may be thinking in these lines of the separated lovers Pyramus and Thisbe, whose story, borrowed from Ovid, Marie parodies in the conclusion of *Les Deus Amanz.*

Chaitivel *(The Unfortunate One)*

It is my desire to bring to mind
a *lai* that I have heard about.
I shall tell you the adventure,
its name, and the city
5   where it was born.
Men call it *The Unfortunate One,*
but there are many
who call it *The Four Sorrows.*

In Brittany, at Nantes, there lived
10 a lady, respected
for her beauty, her education,
and the very best manners.
There wasn't a knight in that land
who had ever done anything praiseworthy,
15 who, if he saw her but once,
did not love and court her.
She could not love them all,
but she didn't want to refuse them either.[1]
It would be better to seek the love
20 of all the ladies in one land
than to separate a single fool from his rag,
for he wants to strike out at once.[2]
The lady grants her favor
according to her goodwill;
25 however, if she doesn't want to hear someone,
she shouldn't abuse him with words
but honor him, hold him dear,

---

1. *reuser,* "refuse," in Warnke's text; *tuer,* "kill," according to both Ewert and Rychner.

2. The courting may be as futile as the attempt to take a worthless object from a fool, but the fool will fight while the lady may accept; meanwhile, presumably, the courting itself can give some pleasure. The passage has never been satisfactorily explained.

serve his pleasure and be grateful.
The lady I wish to tell you of
30 was so sought after in love,
for her beauty and her merit,
that men thought about her day and night.

In Brittany there were four barons
whose names I do not know;
35 they were not very old
but they had great beauty,
and they were brave, valiant knights,
generous, courtly, open-handed;
they were widely esteemed,
40 noble men of that land.
These four loved the lady,
and took pains to do good deeds;
to win her and her love[3]
each did his utmost.
45 Each one sought her for himself,
put all his efforts into his suit.
There was not one who didn't think
that he was doing better than the others.
The lady had good sense:
50 she took her time to consider,
to find out and to ask
which of them it would be best to love.
They were all of such great merit
one could not choose the best.
55 She didn't want to lose three in order to have one,
so she was nice to each of them;
she gave them all tokens of love,
she sent them all messages.
None of them knew about the others;

3. *Pur li e pur s'amur aveir:* the first five words suggest simple love inspiration, "for her and her love," but the last word *aveir* makes it clear that it is for tangible reward, possession of the lady.

60   but no one was able to leave her;
     with his service and his prayers
     each thought he was succeeding.
     At the assembly of knights,
     each one wanted to be first,
65   to do well, if he could,
     in order to please the lady.
     They all considered her their love,
     all carried her token,
     a ring, or sleeve, or banner,
70   and each one cried her name.
     She loved all four and held them all
     until one year, after Easter,
     a tournament was called,
     before the city of Nantes.
75   To meet the four lovers,
     men came from other lands:
     French and Normans,
     Flemish, Brabants,
     Boulognese, Angevins,
80   and near neighbors too.
     All were anxious to go.
     They had stayed there a long time;
     then, on the evening of the tournament,
     they exchanged blows furiously.
85   The four lovers armed,
     left the city;
     their knights followed them,
     but the burden fell on those four.
     Those outside knew them[4]
90   by their tokens and shields;
     they sent knights against them,
     two from Flanders and two from Hainault,
     ready to strike.
     There was no one there who did not want to fight.

4. For purposes of the tournament, the knights were apparently divided into inner and outer armies. Cf. Wolfram's *Parzival*.

95 The four saw them approaching,
   they had no desire to flee.
   Lance lowered, at full speed,
   each one chose his partner.
   They struck with such vehemence
100 that the four outsiders fell.
   The others did not worry about their horses,
   but left them riderless;
   they took their stand against the fallen
   and their knights came to their aid.
105 With their advent, there was a great melee,
   many blows struck with swords.
   The lady was in a tower,
   she knew which were her knights and which their men;
   she saw her lovers helping each other
110 and did not know which one to praise most.

   The tournament began,
   ranks grew and swelled.
   Several times that day
   combat was joined before the gate.
115 Her four lovers fought so well,
   that they won honor beyond all the others,
   until night began to fall
   when they should have separated.
   But they kept on, recklessly,
120 far from their people, and they paid for it.
   For three of them were killed
   and the fourth wounded and hurt:
   the tip of the lance shot through his thigh
   into his body: it came out the other side.
125 They were pierced straight through
   and all four fell.
   Those who struck them dead
   threw their shields onto the ground;
   and grieved for them—
130 they had not meant to kill them.

The noise began and the cries,
such mourning was never heard.
The people from the city came
without a thought for the others.[5]
135 In sorrow for these knights,
two thousand
undid their visors,
drew out their hair and beards;
all felt a common grief.
140 Each one was placed upon his shield
and carried to the city
to the lady he had loved.
As soon as she knew the adventure
she fell, fainting, on the hard ground.
145 When she recovered from her faint,
she mourned for each by name.
"Alas," she said, "what shall I do?
I'll never be happy again.
I loved these four knights
150 and desired each one for himself;
there was great good in all of them;
they loved me more than anything.
For their beauty, their bravery,
their merit, their generosity,
155 I made them fix their love on me;
I didn't want to lose them all by taking one.
I don't know which I should grieve for most;
but I cannot conceal or disguise my grief.
I see one wounded, three are dead;
160 nothing in the world can comfort me.
I shall see that the dead are buried
and if the wounded one can be healed,
I shall willingly undertake it,
and find a good doctor for him."

5. The "others" are the outside, or enemy, knights.

165 She had him brought to her chambers;
    then she had the others prepared
    with great love, nobly
    and richly fitted out.
    She made great offerings and gifts
170 in a very rich abbey
    where they were buried.
    God have mercy on them!
    She sent for wise doctors
    and assigned them to the knight
175 who lay wounded in her chamber
    until he could be healed.
    She went to see him often
    and comforted him gently;
    but she mourned for the other three
180 and suffered great grief for them.
    One summer day, after dinner,
    the lady was talking to the knight;
    then she remembered her great sorrow,
    hid her head and her face,
185 she lost herself in her thoughts.
    He looked at her
    and saw that she was thinking.
    He addressed her in a proper way:
    "Lady, you are upset.
190 What are you thinking? Tell me.
    Give up your sorrow.
    You must find comfort somewhere."
    "Friend," she said, "I was thinking,
    remembering your companions.
195 Never did a lady of my position,
    however beautiful, noble, or wise,
    love four such men at once,
    only to lose them all in a day
    except for you, who were wounded;
200 you were in great danger of dying.

Because I have loved you so,
I want my grief to be remembered:
I shall compose a *lai* about the four of you
and call it *The Four Sorrows!*"
205 When he heard her,
the knight quickly answered:
"Lady, compose the new *lai*
but call it *The Unfortunate One!*
and I'll show you why
210 it should have such a name.
The others have been dead some time;
they spent their lives
in great pain that they suffered
because of their love for you;
215 but I, who escaped alive,
am confused and miserable—
the one I could love most in the world
I see coming and going frequently,
speaking with me morning and evening,
220 but I can have no joy from her,
from kisses or embraces,
nor any other good but talk.
You make me suffer a hundred such ills,
that it would be better for me to die.
225 If the *lai* is to be named for me,
let it be called *The Unfortunate One.*
Whoever calls it *The Four Sorrows*
will be changing its real name."
"By my faith," she said, "I like that.
230 Let's call it *The Unfortunate One.*"
So the *lai* was begun
and then perfected and performed.
Of those who traveled about with it,
some called it *The Four Sorrows;*
235 either name is apt,
both suit the subject.

The Unfortunate One is the common name.
Here it ends, there is no more;
I've heard no more and I know no more about it;
240 I shall tell you no more of it.

❧ CHAITIVEL (*The Unfortunate One*)

IN CHAITIVEL, Marie writes a *lai* about a lady who writes a *lai* about her four lovers, who would have done better to write poetry themselves, instead of fighting, to impress their lady. The *lai* is really about the kind of love found in courtly lyrics: devotion to the ideal and apparently inaccessible lady who is loved by all the worthy men who know her, but particularly by the poet who writes poetry to praise her and at the same time to relieve and describe his own suffering. Marie takes the clichés of lyric poetry to their extremes, and makes fun of the tradition. The *lai* has two names, *Le Chaitivel* (*The Unfortunate One*) and *Les Quatre Dols* (*The Four Sorrows*), not in two languages, as in *Chevrefoil* and *Laustic,* but from two different perspectives, as in *Eliduc,* his and hers. *Chaitivel* is the name given to it by the one surviving lover, to describe his distress. *Quatre Dols* is the lady's name for it, to commemorate her achievement in having won the love of four such men.

The story shows up the futility and perhaps the hypocrisy of the men's love service: three of the four lovers die in a tourney, showing off before the lady and taking excessive risks in order to impress her, and the fourth is badly wounded, probably castrated, and therefore unable to possess her even if she were willing. Tourneys are meant for display: men should not be killed in them; and it is clear in the poem that the knights responsible for the deaths did not intend them, that it was the recklessness of the lovers that brought them about. Thus, for all the talk of their great deeds, their deaths serve no purpose. And, ironically, the one who is left alive might as well be dead for all the satisfaction he gets from the lady. Of course, he does have her daily attention and conversation, which is what courtly lovers pretend to want, but which, in fact, is not enough.

The focus of attention in the *lai,* however, is on the lady, and this in itself is a comment on the lyric tradition, in which the lady is the excuse for the poetry and the apparent subject of it, but in reality has little existence within it. Here Marie's emphasis on the object of all their devotion helps to show up the foolishness of such devotion. The lady is most concerned with her prestige as the inspiration for their love. When they are alive she is concerned with which one would be best for her love (l. 52), which is doing best in the fighting (l. 110), and, when they are dead, which she should grieve for most (l. 157). She was unwilling to choose one of them because that would have meant giving up the other three, so she kept them all, but without letting them know about one another, deceiving them all into thinking they were her favorite. She keeps mourning the loss of the three, remembering that the fourth is still alive only as an afterthought (see lines 197–9), and thinking of him still as one of them (l. 203: "I shall make a *lai* about the four of you" "vus quatre")—hardly flattering or comforting to him. Indeed one wonders if she would have been happier had he also died. She is certainly concerned with the dead, giving them sumptuous funerals and burials, but that is because they enable her to make the most of her own emotions: she composes the *lai* in order to record her love and her grief, not their suffering or death: "Because I loved you so, I want my grief to be remembered" (ll. 201–2). This is another clever twist of the conventional lyric situation, in which the man pretends to write about the lady he loves, but in fact writes about his own emotions, his joy and suffering, his hopes and frustrations.

The *lai* ends with the love situation unresolved, as it usually is in the lyric. Marie repeats four times in the last three lines that there is "no more" to it. We are left to assume that the surviving lover continues to worship the lady without fulfillment, and she to glory in her conquest.

Chevrefoil (*The Honeysuckle*)

I should like very much
to tell you the truth
about the *lai* men call *Chevrefoil*—
why it was composed and where it came from.
5 Many have told and recited it to me
 and I have found it in writing,
about Tristan and the queen
and their love that was so true,
that brought them much suffering
10 and caused them to die the same day.
King Mark was annoyed,
angry at his nephew Tristan;
he exiled Tristan from his land
because of the queen whom he loved.
15 Tristan returned to his own country,
South Wales, where he was born,
he stayed a whole year;
he couldn't come back.
Afterward he began to expose himself
20 to death and destruction.
Don't be surprised at this:
for one who loves very faithfully
is sad and troubled
when he cannot satisfy his desires.
25 Tristan was sad and worried,
so he set out from his land.
He traveled straight to Cornwall,
where the queen lived,
and entered the forest all alone—
30 he didn't want anyone to see him;
he came out only in the evening
when it was time to find shelter.
He took lodging that night,
with peasants, poor people.

35 He asked them for news
    of the king—what he was doing.
    They told him they had heard
    that the barons had been summoned by ban.
    They were to come to Tintagel
40 where the king wanted to hold his court;
    at Pentecost they would all be there,
    there'd be much joy and pleasure,
    and the queen would be there too.
    Tristan heard and was very happy;
45 she would not be able to go there
    without his seeing her pass.
    The day the king set out,
    Tristan also came to the woods
    by the road he knew
50 their assembly must take.
    He cut a hazel tree in half,
    then he squared it.
    When he had prepared the wood,
    he wrote his name on it with his knife.
55 If the queen noticed it—
    and she should be on the watch for it,
    for it had happened before
    and she had noticed it then—
    she'd know when she saw it,
60 that the piece of wood had come from her love.
    This was the message of the writing[1]
    that he had sent to her:
    he had been there a long time,
    had waited and remained

---

1. There are several possible explanations of this line: that Tristan had sent a message to her before she arrived in the forest, which seems least likely since it is not otherwise mentioned; that his name on the wood told her everything because of the understanding that existed between them; that the message was written on the wood in runic inscriptions which only the specially trained could read (see M. Cagnon, *"Chievrefoil* and the Ogamic Tradition," *Romania* 91 [1970], 238–55).

65 to find out and to discover
how he could see her,
for he could not live without her.
With the two of them it was just
as it is with the honeysuckle
70 that attaches itself to the hazel tree:
when it has wound and attached
and worked itself around the trunk,
the two can survive together;
but if someone tries to separate them,
75 the hazel dies quickly
and the honeysuckle with it.
"Sweet love, so it is with us:
You cannot live without me, nor I without you."
The queen rode along;
80 she looked at the hillside
and saw the piece of wood; she knew what it was,
she recognized all the letters.
The knights who were accompanying her,
who were riding with her,
85 she ordered to stop:
she wanted to dismount and rest.
They obeyed her command.
She went far away from her people
and called her girl
90 Brenguein, who was loyal to her.
She went a short distance from the road;
and in the woods she found him
whom she loved more than any living thing.
They took great joy in each other.
95 He spoke to her as much as he desired,
she told him whatever she liked.
Then she assured him
that he would be reconciled with the king—
for it weighed on him
100 that he had sent Tristan away;

he'd done it because of the accusation.
Then she departed, she left her love,
but when it came to the separation,
they began to weep.
105 Tristan went to Wales,
to wait until his uncle sent for him.
For the joy that he'd felt
from his love when he saw her,
by means of the stick he inscribed
110 as the queen had instructed,
and in order to remember the words,
Tristan, who played the harp well,
composed a new *lai* about it.
I shall name it briefly:
115 in English they call it *Goat's Leaf*
the French call it *Chevrefoil*.
I have given you the truth
about the *lai* that I have told here.

CHEVREFOIL (*The Honeysuckle*)

CHEVREFOIL presents one moment of the famous love story of
Tristan and Isolt—a meeting in the woods, a moment that has
little importance in longer versions of the story. Marie repeats
a motif from an earlier episode of the Tristan legend, the name
written on a piece of wood as a secret signal between the lovers,
but transposes it from the intrigue of a rendezvous in the early
period of their affair to a reunion after a long and painful sep-
aration. Marie alludes to a number of details in the story that
her audience would recognize: the king's anger over the affair,
the envious barons, and the loyal servant Brenguein, all of
which evoke the world that was hostile to the love. She makes
no reference to the potion, either because it is too obvious to

mention or, more likely, because she is emphasizing a different aspect of their love: not the fatal passion that binds their lives together, like the honeysuckle and the hazel tree that cannot live when separated, but the perfect understanding and joy they share when they are together, and which sustain them when they are apart.

In a sense, Marie has substituted the natural image of the honeysuckle for that of the magic love potion to explain the binding nature of the love, the mutual dependence which draws them together despite all the obstacles the world sets in their way; but what she emphasizes in the *lai* is the joy of the moment of reunion, the one happy moment in lives that are not only filled with sorrow but destined to end tragically. Although Marie allows the lovers to look forward to a formal reconciliation with the king—to live on that hope—we know it will never occur because she has told us that they will die on the same day. But she chooses to show us what she considers the essence of a love that is the subject of one of the most popular romances of the Middle Ages: the understanding and sensitivity that sets the two lovers apart from others and enables Tristan to leave a sign that only Isolt will see and comprehend; and the deep affection that makes a snatched moment of conversation a joyful scene of love. That essence is the "truth" Marie assures us she is telling at the beginning and the end of the *lai*, which is the same whether the story is told in English, and called *Goteslef*, or in French, and called *Chevrefoil*. It is what Tristan captures in the *lai* he composes for himself to remember that meeting, and it is what Marie preserves in the *lai* she composes for us.

Finally, perhaps, it is only art that can capture such perfect love and joy in life, which, in earlier *lais*, seemed to issue from the imagination of the lover when it existed, and in the last *lai*, *Eliduc*, will be real and permanent only in the love of God. If Marie means that such love as she describes in *Chevrefoil* is only possible in the mind of the lover, that may explain why, in a *lai* that makes much of mutual feeling and that draws on a tradition in which Isolt is a major force in the story, Marie does not even name the heroine; she simply calls her "the queen," the title which, because it reminds us of her position and responsibility, also tells us how impossible their love must be in the world.

Eliduc

I shall tell you, as I understand
the truth of it, and as I know it,
a very old Breton *lai,*
its story and all its substance.
5 In Brittany there was a knight,
brave and courtly, bold and proud;
Eliduc was his name, it seems to me,
no man in the country was more valiant.
He had a wife, noble and wise,
10 of high birth, of good family.
They lived together a long time
and loved each other loyally;
but then, because of a war,
he went to seek service elsewhere.[1]
15 There, he fell in love with a girl,
the daughter of a king and a queen.
Guilliadun was her name,
no girl in the kingdom was more beautiful.
Eliduc's wife was called
20 Guildeluec in her country.
From these two the *lai* is named
Guildeluec and Gualadun.[2]
At first the *lai* was called *Eliduc,*
but now the name has been changed,
25 for it happened to the women.
The adventure behind the *lai,*
I shall relate to you, as it occurred,
and I shall tell you the truth.

Eliduc had a lord,
30 a king of Brittany,

---

1. *soudees quere* literally means to hire himself out to fight for a lord in
return for pay and maintenance. I am translating *soudees* as "service" through-
out the *lai,* and *soudeur* as "soldier."

2. The spelling of the name in the alternate title differs from the name of
the character as it is otherwise given in the *lai* (*Guilliadun*).

who loved and cherished him—
Eliduc served him loyally.
Whenever the king had to travel,
Eliduc guarded the land for him;
35 he was retained because of his valor.
Much good came to him from that:
he could hunt in the forests,
there was no forester bold enough
to dare try and stop him,
40 nor did one ever grumble about it.
But envy of his success,
which often happens among people,
caused trouble between him and his lord.
He was slandered and accused
45 until the lord sent him away from his court
without a formal accusation.
Eliduc did not know why.
He asked the king many times
to listen to his defense,
50 not to believe the slander,
for he'd always served the king willingly;
but the king would not respond.
Since he would hear none of it,
Eliduc had to leave.
55 He went to his home
and sent for all his friends;
Eliduc told them all about the king, his lord,
about the anger he now showed toward him;
he had served him as well as he was able
60 and did not deserve the king's ill will.
The peasant proverb says,
when it admonishes the ploughman,
that the love of a lord is not a fief:
he is wise and clever
65 who gives loyalty to his lord,
and love to his good neighbors.

Eliduc doesn't want to remain in the country
but will, he says, cross the sea;
he will go to the kingdom of Logres,
70 where he will enjoy himself for a while.
He will leave his wife at home [in his own land]
commending her to his men,
to guard her loyally,
and to all his friends as well.
75 With that counsel he stopped,
and attired himself richly.
His friends were very sad
because he was leaving them.
Eliduc took ten knights along,
80 his wife escorted him,
revealing enormous sorrow
at her husband's departure.
But he assured Guildeluec
that he would be faithful to her.
85 Then he departed,
and began his journey straightaway;
he came to the sea, crossed it,
and arrived at Totnes.
Several kings in that land
90 were fighting among themselves.
Near Exeter, in that country,
there was a very powerful man,
old and ancient.
He had no male heir of his own flesh,
95 but a daughter of marriageable age.
Because he did not want to give her
to his peer, the latter made war on him,
laying waste his whole land.
He had cut him off inside a castle;
100 no man in the castle was so bold
that he dared go out against him,
dared meet him in battle or in combat.

Eliduc heard about it;
he didn't want to go any farther,
105 since he had found a war.
He wanted to remain in that country.
To the king who was most pressed
and injured and hurt,
he'd give all the help within his power
110 and remain in that king's service.
He sent his messengers
and informed him, by letter,
that he had left his country,
that he had come to help him.
115 The king should make his pleasure known by return messenger
and, if he did not want to have him,
he should grant him an escort through his land;
Eliduc would travel farther to seek service.
When the king saw the messengers,
120 he loved and cherished them.
He called his constable,
commanded him quickly
to prepare an escort
and bring the baron to him,
125 and to have lodgings made ready
for him and his men to stay in,
and to give them
as much as they might want to spend in a month.
The escort was prepared
130 and sent for Eliduc,
who was received with great honor—
exceedingly welcome to the king.
His lodging was with a bourgeois,
who was very wise and courtly;
135 his lovely, curtained room
he turned over to his guest.
Eliduc had himself well served
and invited to his dinner
the poor knights

140 who were lodged in the town.
He forbade all his men
to be so bold,
in the first forty days,
as to take any gifts or money.
145 On the third day that he was there,
the cry was raised in the city
that their enemies had arrived
and had spread throughout the countryside;
they wanted to assail the city,
150 to reach its gates.
Eliduc heard the noise,
the populace in confusion.
He armed himself without delay
and his companions did the same.
155 Fourteen mounted knights
were staying in the city—
several were wounded,
many were prisoners—
they saw Eliduc mount;
160 they went to arm at their lodgings
and rode out the gate with him,
without awaiting a summons.
"Sire," they said, "we'll go with you
and whatever you do we shall do."
165 He answered: "I thank you.
Does any one of you
know a narrow spot or ambush
where we can stop them?
If we wait for them here,
170 it may be that we shall joust,
but that serves no purpose;
there must be another way."
They tell him: "Sire, in faith,
near this wood, in that thicket,
175 there is a narrow cart road

by which they return
when they've taken their booty;
they'll return that way,
unarmed on their mounts;
180 they ride back often
and risk the chance
of dying outright."
We could swiftly damage them,
injure and hurt them there.
185 Eliduc said to them: "Friends,
I pledge you my faith:
who does not often go
where he may expect to suffer a loss
will never gain anything,
190 never win great renown.
You are all the king's men,
and owe him great faith.
Come with me where I go,
do what I do.
195 I assure you, faithfully,
you will come to no harm
as long as I can help.
If we can gain anything there,
it will win us great fame
200 to have hurt our enemies."
They accepted his assurance
and led him to the wood;
they hid themselves near the road
until the others returned.
205 Eliduc showed them everything,
instructed and planned
in what way they would ride against them,
how they would shout.
When they had entered the pass,
210 Eliduc shouted at them.
He called all his companions

and exhorted them to do well.
They struck hard,
spared nothing.
215 The others were completely surprised,
quickly routed and dispersed,
conquered, in a short time.
Their constable was captured
and many other knights;
220 they were all entrusted to the squires.
There were twenty-five of them
and they captured thirty of the others.
They also took armor to their profit.
They made exceptional gains there
225 and came back very happy:
they had done very well.
The king was in a tower,
in great fear for his men;
he complained about Eliduc,
230 he thought and feared
that he had endangered
his knights in order to betray them.
The knights were approaching in a crowd
all burdened and loaded down.
235 There were many more returning
than had gone out;
that's why the king didn't know them,
why he doubted and suspected.
He commanded the gates to be shut,
240 told the people to mount the walls
to shoot and throw things at the knights;
but there will be no need for that.
They had sent
a squire ahead, riding hard,
245 to tell them the adventure
all about the new soldier,
how he conquered the others,

and how he behaved;
there was never such a knight.
250 He captured their constable,
took twenty-nine others,
and wounded and killed many more.
The king, when he heard the news,
rejoiced wonderfully.
255 He descended from the tower
and went to meet Eliduc.
He thanked him for his deeds.
Eliduc turned the prisoners over to the king,
then he divided the booty among the others;
260 for his own use he kept only three horses,
which were allotted to him;
he divided and gave everything,
his own share as well,
to the prisoners and the men.
265 After the feat that I have described to you,
the king loved and cherished Eliduc.
He kept him a whole year—
and those who had come with him—
and accepted his oath of loyalty;
270 he made him protector of his land.
Eliduc was courtly and wise,
a handsome knight, brave and generous.
The king's daughter heard him spoken of,
his virtues described.
275 Through one of her trusted chamberlains
she asked Eliduc, begged and summoned him
to come visit her,
to speak with her and become acquainted;
she was quite astonished
280 that he had not come.
Eliduc answered that he would go,
that he would willingly make her acquaintance.
He mounted his horse,
taking one knight with him,

285 and went to speak to the girl.
When he was about to enter the chamber,
he sent the chamberlain ahead.
Eliduc delayed somewhat,
until the other returned.

290 With a sweet look, with a simple expression,
and with very noble behavior,
he spoke politely;
he thanked the girl,
Guilliadun, who was very lovely,

295 that she had been pleased to summon him
to come and speak with her.
She took him by the hand
and they sat on a bed,
they spoke of many things.

300 She looked at him intently,
at his face, his body, his appearance;
she said to herself there was nothing unpleasant about him.
She greatly admired him in her heart.
Love sent her a message,

305 commanding her to love him,
that made her go pale and sigh
but she didn't want to speak of it
in case he might hold it against her.
He stayed there a long time;

310 then took his leave and went away;
she gave the leave most unwillingly,
nonetheless he left
and returned to his lodging.
He was gloomy and worried,

315 concerned about the lovely girl,
the daughter of his lord, the king,
because she had summoned him so sweetly,
because she had sighed.
He thought it unfair

320 that he'd been so long in the country
and had not seen her often.

But when he said that, he was sorry;
for he remembered his wife
and how he had assured her
325 that he'd be faithful to her,
that he'd conduct himself loyally.
The girl who had seen him
wanted to make him her lover.
She'd never thought so well of anyone;
330 if she could, she would have him.
All night she was awake,
she couldn't rest or sleep.
The next day, in the morning, she got up
and went to a window;
335 she summoned her chamberlain,
and revealed her condition to him.
"By my faith," she said, "this is terrible.
I have gotten myself into a sorry mess.
I love the new soldier,
340 Eliduc, the good knight.
Last night I had no rest,
I couldn't close my eyes to sleep.
If he wants to give me his love[3]
and promise his person to me,
345 I shall do whatever he likes;
great good will come to him:
he will be the king of this land.
He is so wise and courtly
that, if he does not love me with real love,
350 I must die in great sorrow.
When she had said what she wished,
the chamberlain she'd called
gave loyal advice;
no one should criticize him for it.

---

3. The expression Guilliadun uses throughout this passage is *par amur amer*, "to love with love," presumably with passion, desire, not just as a vassal would his lord's daughter.

355 "Lady," he said, "since you love him,
send something to him,
a belt, a ribbon, or a ring;
send it, he will like that.
If he receives it well,
360 if he is happy that you sent it,
you may be sure of his love.
There is no emperor on earth,
who, if you wanted to love him,
should not be happy [to have your love]."
365 When she heard his advice
the girl answered:
"How can I know from my present
if he has any desire to love me?
I've never seen a knight
370 who had to be begged—
whether he loved or hated—
who would not willingly take
a present that was offered to him.
I would hate to have him make fun of me.
375 But still, by a reaction
one can know something.
Get ready, then, and go to him."
"I am," he said, "all ready."
"You will bring him a gold ring
380 and give him my belt.
You will greet him a thousand times in my name."
The chamberlain left.
She remained in such a state
that she almost called him back;
385 but she let him go
and then began to carry on:
"Oh, how my heart was assaulted
by a man from a strange land.
I don't even know if he is nobly born,
390 he left so quickly.
I shall remain in grief.

I've fixed my desires foolishly.
I never spoke to him before yesterday
and now I'm asking for his love.
395 I think he will blame me;
but if he is courtly, he will be grateful.
Now everything is up to chance [*aventure*].
And if he has no interest in my love,
I shall be miserable,
400 never in my life shall I have any joy."
While she was carrying on,
the chamberlain was moving quickly.
He came to Eliduc
and greeted him in secret
405 with what the girl had sent;
he presented the ring
and gave him the belt.
The knight thanked him.
He put the gold ring on his finger
410 pulled the belt around him;
the youth said no more,
nor did Eliduc ask anything,
except that he offered him something of his.
But the chamberlain took nothing and departed;
415 he returned to his mistress,
whom he found in her chamber;
he brought her Eliduc's greeting
and his thanks for the present.
"Come, now," she said, "don't hide anything from me.
420 Does he really want to love me?"
He answered: "So it seems to me.
The knight is not frivolous;
I find him courtly and wise,
one who knows how to hide his feelings.
425 I brought him your greetings
and presented your things.
He put on your belt,
pulled it tight around him;

he placed your ring on his finger.
430 I said nothing more to him nor he to me."
"He didn't receive it as a love token?
If that is so, I am betrayed."
He told her, "By my faith, I don't know,
but listen to what I have to say:
435 if he didn't really wish you well,
he wouldn't want anything of yours."
"You are," she said, "making fun of me.
I know perfectly well that he doesn't hate me.
I've never done him any harm
440 except that I love him so intensely;
if he hates me nonetheless,
then he ought to die.
Never, through you or anyone else,
until I speak to him myself,
445 do I want to ask him for anything;
I want to show him myself
how love for him tortures me.
But I don't know if he'll remain."
The chamberlain answered:
450 "Lady, the king holds him
by an oath until a year from now—
that he will serve the king loyally.
You'll have sufficient time
to show him what you please."
455 When she heard that Eliduc would remain,
she was filled with joy,
very happy about Eliduc's remaining.
She knew nothing of the distress
he felt since he'd seen her.
460 He had no joy or pleasure
except when he thought of her.
But he considered himself unfortunate
because, before he left his own country,
he had promised his wife
465 that he'd love no one but her.

His heart was now in great turmoil.
He wanted to keep his faith,
but he couldn't keep himself
from loving the girl,
470 Guilliadun, who was so lovely,
or from seeing and addressing,
kissing and embracing her;
but he would not pursue the love
that would dishonor her
475 because of the faith he owed his wife
and because he served the king.
Eliduc was in great distress.
He mounted with no more delay,
calling his companions to him.
480 At the castle he went to speak to the king:
he would see the girl if he could—
that's the reason he bestirred himself.
The king had gotten up from dinner
and entered his daughter's chambers.
485 He began to play chess
with a knight from overseas
who, on the other side of the chess board,
was teaching his daughter.[4]
Eliduc went forward;
490 The king received him well
and sat him down beside him.
He called his daughter and said:
"Young lady, you should certainly
know this knight,
495 and show him great honor;
in five hundred there is none better."
When the girl heard
what her father commanded,
she was very happy.

4. Chess is often an allegory of the love game. Note that Guilliadun is
learning to play from a stranger.

500 She rose and called Eliduc,
    they sat down far from the others;
    both were fired with love.
    She didn't dare broach the subject
    and he was afraid to speak,
505 except to thank her
    for the present she had sent:
    he'd never had anything more precious.
    She answered the knight
    saying that she was very pleased,
510 that was why she'd sent the ring
    and the belt as well,
    for he had taken possession of her being.
    She loved him with such love
    that she wanted to make him her lord;
515 and if she could not have him,
    he could be sure of one thing:
    she would never have a living man.
    Now let him tell her his desire.
    "Lady," he said, "I am very grateful to you
520 for your love, it gives me great joy.
    Since you hold me in such high esteem,
    I must be happy.
    I shall not forget it.
    I've been retained by the king for one year;
525 he has accepted my pledge,
    I shall not leave him under any condition
    until the war is over.
    Then I shall return to my country
    if I can get your leave,
530 because I don't want to remain."
    The girl answered:
    "Love, I thank you.
    You are so wise and courtly,
    by then you will have decided
535 what you want to do with me.
    I love and trust you more than anything."

They made their pledges to each other;
they spoke no more that time.
Eliduc went to his lodging;
540 he was filled with joy, he had done well.
He was often able to speak to his love,
there was great affection between them.
Meanwhile he took such pains with the war
that he captured and held
545 the one who was waging war on the king
and set the whole land free.
He was highly respected for his bravery,
his wisdom, and his generosity;
everything went well for him.
550 Within the term [of his service]
the king of Brittany sent to find him[5]
three messengers from his land:
he was being hard pressed and hurt,
damaged and harmed;
555 he was losing all his castles
and his land was being laid waste.
He had often been sorry
that Eliduc had left him;
he'd been badly advised,
560 he'd been wrong about him.
The traitors who accused Eliduc,
slandered and made trouble for him,
the king had thrown out of the country
and sent into exile for ever.
565 Because of his great need, he was sending for Eliduc,
summoning and begging him—
in the name of the alliance that bound them
when the king received homage from Eliduc—
to come and help him,
570 for the king needed him badly.
Eliduc heard the news.

5. This is the lord who had exiled him at the beginning of the story.

He was upset because of the girl;
for he loved her painfully
and she him, as much as one could.
575 But there was no folly between them,
no frivolity, no shame:
When they were together,
their lovemaking consisted
of courting and speaking
580 and giving fine gifts.
This was her intention and her hope:
she thought to have him completely
and to hold him, if she could;
she didn't know he had a wife.
585 "Alas," he said, "I have acted very badly.
I have been in this country too long.
If only I had never seen this land.
I have loved a girl here—
Guilliadun, the king's daughter—
590 very much, and she me.
If I have to leave her,
one of us must die,
or perhaps both.
Nonetheless, I have to go;
595 my lord has sent for me by letter
appealed to me by my oath
and my wife, too, for her part.
Now I must be careful.
Certainly, I can not remain,
600 I am forced of necessity to go.
If I were to marry my love,
Christianity would not allow it.
This is bad in every way.
God, how hard it is to part.
605 But whoever may blame me for it,
I shall always do right by her;
I shall do whatever she wills,
act as she advises.

The king, her lord, has a secure peace,
610 I don't think anyone will make war with him again.
For my own lord's need
I shall ask for leave before the day
fixed by my term
for me to remain here.
615 I shall go and speak to the girl,
reveal my situation to her;
she will tell me her wish
and I shall do it, as far as I can."
The knight waited no longer,
620 he went to get his leave from the king.
He told and related the adventure to him,
showed and read him the letter
his lord had sent,
by which, in his distress, he had summoned Eliduc.
625 The king heard the summons
and that he would not remain;
he was very sad and disturbed.
He offered much of what he had,
a third of his inheritance
630 and the whole of his treasure;
to keep him, the king would do so much for him
that Eliduc would praise him forever.
"By God," he said, "this time,
since my lord is harassed
635 and has summoned me from so far,
I must go to help him in his need;
I cannot remain, no matter what.
But if you need my service,
I shall willingly return to you
640 with a great force of knights."
For that the king thanked him
and graciously gave him leave.
All the possessions of his household
the king put at his disposal,
645 gold and silver, dogs and horses,

and cloth of silk, good and fine.
Eliduc took in moderation;
then he said, in a fitting way,
that if it pleased the king
650 he would go and speak most willingly with his daughter.
The king answered: "That pleases me very much."
He sent a boy ahead
to open the chamber door for him.
Eliduc went to speak to her.
655 When she saw him, she called him,
greeted him six thousand times.
He consulted her about his affairs,
and briefly revealed the news of his journey.
Before he'd told her everything,
660 taken or asked for her leave,
she fainted in sorrow
and lost all her color.
When Eliduc saw her faint
he began to lose his mind;
665 he kissed her mouth again and again
and wept quite tenderly;
he took her and held her in his arms,
until she recovered from her faint.
"By God," he said, "my sweet love,
670 listen to me for a little:
You are my life and my death,
in you is all my comfort.
That's why I am consulting you,
because there is an understanding between us.
675 I am returning to my country out of necessity.
I have taken my leave of your father,
but I shall do what you wish
whatever may come of it."
"Take me," she said, "with you,
680 since you don't want to remain.
If you don't, I shall kill myself;
I will never have joy or good."

Eliduc answered gently
that he loved her with good love:
685 "Sweet, in truth I am pledged
by my word to your father—
if I took you with me
I would betray my faith to him—
until my term is over.
690 I swear and pledge loyally to you:
if you want to give me leave
and set a time and name a day,
if you want me to come back,
there is nothing in the world that will stop me
695 as long as I am alive and healthy;
my life is completely in your hands."
She had great love for him;
she gave him a term and named the day
for him to come and take her.
700 There was great sorrow when they parted;
they exchanged gold rings
and kissed each other sweetly.
He went as far as the sea;
the wind was good, he crossed it quickly.
705 When Eliduc returned,
his lord was joyful and happy
his friends and his relatives
and all the others too,
above all his good wife,
710 who was very lovely, wise, and worthy.
But he was always preoccupied
because of the love that had seized him.
Nothing that he saw
gave him joy or a happy look,
715 he would never have joy
until he saw his love.
He behaved furtively.
His wife had a heavy heart,
she didn't know why this was;

720 and worried about it to herself.
She asked him often
if he'd heard from anyone
that she had done something wrong
while he was out of the country;
725 she would willingly defend herself
before his people, whenever he desired.
"Lady," he said, "I don't accuse you
of any fault or misdeed.
But in the country where I stayed,
730 I pledged and swore to the king
that I would return to him;
for he has great need of me.
If the king, my lord, were at peace,
I would leave within a week.
735 I should have to endure great hardship
before I could come back.
Indeed, until I return
I can find no joy in anything I see
because I don't want to betray my faith."
740 Then the lady left him alone.
Eliduc was with his lord;
he had helped him and had been of great use to him.
The king followed his advice
as he kept watch over the whole country.
745 But when the time
that the girl had set approached,
he undertook to make peace;
he reconciled all the king's enemies.
Then he prepared to travel [on his own]
750 and chose the people he would take.
He took two of his nephews, whom he very much loved,
and one of his chamberlains—
the one who knew the situation,
who had carried his messages—
755 and his squires only;

he didn't want anyone else.
He had them pledge and swear
to keep his whole affair secret.
He put to sea without delay,
760 crossed it quickly,
and arrived in the country
where he was so eagerly awaited.
Eliduc was very clever:
he took lodging far from the harbor;
765 he didn't want to be seen,
or found or recognized.
He prepared his chamberlain
and sent him to his love,
to tell her that he had come,
770 that he had kept his promise.
At night, when it was dark,
she should leave the city;
the chamberlain would go with her
and he would meet her.
775 The chamberlain had changed all his clothes;
he went slowly on foot
straight to the city
where the king's daughter was.
He asked and sought
780 until he got inside her room.
He greeted the girl
and told her that her love had come.
Before she heard the news
she was gloomy and troubled,
785 then she wept tenderly for joy
and kissed him often.
The chamberlain told her that in the evening
she was to go with him.
All day they stayed there
790 and planned their journey carefully.
At night, when it was dark,

they left the city,
the youth and the girl,
only those two.
795 She was very much afraid that someone would see her.
She was dressed in a silk gown,
finely embroidered with gold,
and wrapped in a short cloak.
Far from the gate, the distance of an arrow shot,
800 there was an enclosed wood.
Waiting for them beneath the hedge
was her love, who had just arrived.
The chamberlain brought her,
Eliduc dismounted and kissed her.
805 Their joy at meeting was great.
He helped her mount a horse,
mounted himself, took her rein,
and went off quickly with her.
They came to the harbor at Totnes
810 and entered a boat immediately;
there was no one there except his men
and his love Guilliadun.
They had good wind
and good weather.
815 But when they were about to arrive,
a storm broke out at sea—
a wind rose before them,
driving them far from the harbor;
it broke and split their mast
820 and tore their sail.
They called on God devoutly,
on Saint Nicholas and Saint Clement,
and on my lady Saint Mary,
to seek help from her son
825 to save them from dying
and let them reach the harbor.
One hour backwards, another forwards,

they moved along the coast;
they were on the verge of shipwreck.
830 Then one of the sailors, loudly,
cried: "What are we doing?
Sire, you have inside with you
the one who is causing our deaths.
We'll never reach land.
835 You already have a faithful wife
but you're bringing another back
in defiance of God and the law
of right and of faith.
Let us throw her into the sea,
840 so we can get home safely."
Eliduc heard what he said
and almost went mad with anger.
"Son of a bitch," he said, "rotten,
filthy traitor, be silent!
845 If you had let my love go
I'd have made you pay for it."
But he held her in his arms
and comforted her as well as he could
from the distress she felt from the sea[6]
850 and from what she'd heard
of her lover having a wife
other than herself in his country.
She fell faint on her face,
all pale and without color.
855 And she remained in a faint
without recovering or sighing.
He who was bringing her back with him
really thought that she was dead.
His grief was terrible; he got up,
860 moved swiftly toward the sailor,

6. Her distress from the sea, *mal . . . en mer*, probably involves a pun on
amer to love, as in Chrétien's *Cligès* and Gottfried's *Tristan*, the latter pre-
sumably from Thomas.

and struck him so hard with an oar
that he knocked him down.
He grabbed his feet and threw him overboard;
the waves carried the body away.
865 After Eliduc had tossed him into the sea,
he took over the helm.
He continued to pilot the boat
until he reached the harbor and brought it to land.
When they arrived,
870 they lowered the gangplank and dropped anchor.
She was still unconscious
and appeared to be dead.
Eliduc was very unhappy;
if he could have had his way, he would have died with her.
875 He asked his companions
what advice each could give him
about where to take the girl;
for he would not leave her
until she was buried,
880 and laid with great honor, with a fine service,
in a consecrated cemetery.
She was the daughter of a king and had a right to that.
They were all confused,
had no advice to give.
885 Eliduc began to consider
where he might take her.
His home was close to the sea,
he could be there for dinner.
There was a forest around it,
890 thirty leagues long,[7]
where a holy hermit lived,
and there was a chapel.
He'd been there forty years;
Eliduc had often spoken with him.
895 He would, he said, bring Guilliadun to him,

7. About ninety miles.

and bury her in the chapel;
he would give enough of his land
to found an abbey
and would establish a convent of monks,
900   or of nuns or canons,
who would always pray for her.
God have mercy on her!
He had his horse brought to him,
commanded all his men to mount.
905   But he had them all swear
not to betray him.
Before him on his palfrey
he carried his love.
He traveled straight along the road
910   until they entered the wood.
They came to the chapel,
called out and beat on the door;
they found no one to answer them
or to open the door.
915   Eliduc had one of his men make his way in,
to open and unlock the door.
Eight days before, the perfect,
the holy, hermit had died.
He found the new tomb;
920   he was very sad, quite dismayed.
The men wanted to dig a grave
in which he might bury his friend,
but he made them hold back.[8]
He told them: "That won't do.
925   First I must seek the advice
of the wise people of the land,
to learn how I can glorify a place
with an abbey or a church.
We shall lay her before the altar
930   and commend her to God."

---

8. I have reversed the order of these two lines.

He had cloths brought
and a bed made up immediately.
The girl was placed on it
and left there for dead.
935 But when it came to leaving,
he thought he would die of grief.
He kissed her eyes and her face.
"Lovely one," he said, "may God never
let me bear arms again
940 or live or endure in the world.
Lovely friend, to your harm you saw me,
sweet love, to your harm you followed me.
Lovely one, if you had been queen,
the love, with which you loved me faithfully,
945 could have been no more loyal and true.
My heart is filled with sorrow because of you.
The day I bury you
I shall become a monk;
each day on your tomb
950 I shall make my grief resound."
Then he left the girl,
shut the door of the chapel.
He sent a messenger
to his home, to announce
955 to his wife that he was coming
but that he was exhausted and upset.
When she heard [that he was coming] she was very happy,
she prepared herself for him
and received her lord well.
960 But little joy awaited her,
for he never showed a pleasant countenance,
never said a good word.
No one dared to speak to him about it.
He was in the house two days;
965 then he heard Mass early in the morning
and set out on the road.

In the wood he went to the chapel
where the girl lay.
He found her unconscious:
970　she did not recover or sigh.
It seemed a great wonder to him
that she was still white and red;
she never lost her color
except that she was a bit paler.
975　He wept in anguish
and prayed for her soul.
When he had said his prayer,
he returned home.
One day when he left the church
980　his wife had him watched
by one of her valets; to him she promised a great deal
if he went and saw from afar
which way his lord turned;
she would give him horses and arms.
985　He did as she commanded.
He went to the woods and followed Eliduc
so that he was not noticed.
He watched well, saw
how he entered the chapel;
990　he heard the sorrow Eliduc gave vent to.
Before Eliduc came out again,
the valet had returned to his lady.
He related everything he heard,
the grief and the noise and the cries
995　of her lord in the hermitage.
Her heart was quite moved.
The lady said: "Let us go right away.
We will search the whole hermitage.
My lord must, I think, travel;
1000　he is going to court to speak to the king.
The hermit died a while ago—
I know that Eliduc loved him

but he wouldn't do that for him,
he wouldn't show such grief."
1005 That's how she left it that time.

That very day, after noon,
Eliduc went to speak to the king.
His wife took the valet with her
and brought him to the hermitage.
1010 When she entered the chapel
and saw the bed of the girl,
who resembled a new rose,
she uncovered her,
saw the body so slender,
1015 the long arms and white hands,
slim fingers, long and smooth;
now she knew the truth,
the reason her lord had felt such grief.
She called the valet
1020 and showed him the wonderful sight.
"Do you see," she said, "this woman
whose beauty resembles a jewel?
This is my lord's love
for whom he feels such grief.
1025 By my faith, I'm not surprised,
if such a lovely woman has perished.
As much for pity as for love
I shall never have joy again."
She began to weep
1030 and to mourn for the girl.
As she sat, weeping, before the bed,
a weasel came running;
it had come out from beneath the altar
and the valet had hit it
1035 because it ran over the body;
he killed it with a stick.
Then he threw it on the floor.

In very little time
her mate ran up[9]

1040 and saw where she lay;
he went around her head
prodded her several times with his foot.
When he couldn't get her up,
he gave signs of grieving.

1045 He left the chapel
and went to the wood for herbs;
he took a flower in his teeth,
a red one,
and came back quickly;

1050 he put it in such a way
inside his companion's mouth,
whom the valet had killed,
that she revived at once.
The lady watched it all,

1055 she cried to the valet: "Hold her.
Throw something, good man, she mustn't get away."
And he threw, striking her
so that the flower fell.
The lady got up and retrieved it

1060 and went back quickly.
Inside the girl's mouth
she placed the very lovely flower.
After a short while
Guilliadun revived and sighed;

1065 then she spoke and opened her eyes.
"God," she said, "I've slept so long."
When the lady heard her speak

9. I use the masculine and feminine pronouns here where it is important to show the relationship of the weasels, not before where it might have led to confusion with the humans in the scene. It is difficult not to make a connection between the episode of the weasels and the main plot, though one hesitates to carry it too far. The lover who grieves for his dead mate seems to represent Eliduc, but the "flower" *he* finds to bring her back to life is his wife's charity.

she began to thank God.
She asked who she was
1070 and the girl replied:
"Lady, I was born in Logres,
the daughter of that country's king.
I have loved a knight very much,
Eliduc, the good soldier;
1075 he brought me here with him.
But he sinned when he deceived me:
he had a wife, but he didn't tell me
or ever give me any idea about that.
When I heard about his wife
1080 I fainted from the grief.
Villainously, he has abandoned me,
friendless, in a strange land.
He has betrayed me, I don't know why.
Whoever believes in a man is very foolish."
1085 "Lovely one," the lady answered,
"there is no living thing in all the world
that can give him joy;
I can assure you of that.
He thinks that you are dead
1090 and is quite disconsolate.
Each day he has come to look at you;
I think he found you unconscious.
I am his wife, in truth,
I have a very heavy heart for his sake,
1095 because of his grief.
I wanted to know where he was going:
I came after him, that's how I found you.
That you are alive gives me great joy;
I shall take you with me
1100 and give you back to your love.
I want to leave him completely free,
and I shall take the veil."
The lady so comforted the girl
that she finally took her away with her.

1105 She had her valet make ready
   and sent him for her lord.
   He traveled until he found him;
   he greeted him fittingly
   and told him the adventure.
1110 Eliduc mounted a horse
   without waiting for any companion.
   By night he had reached home.
   When he found his love alive
   He thanked his wife sweetly.
1115 Eliduc was very pleased,
   he had never been so happy;
   he kissed the girl again and again
   and she him, very sweetly;
   together they felt great joy.
1120 When the lady saw how they looked,
   she addressed her lord;
   she sought and asked his leave
   to depart from him,
   she wanted to be a nun, to serve God.
1125 Let him give her a piece of his land
   to establish an abbey;
   then let him take Guilliadun, whom he so loved,
   for it is neither good nor fitting
   to keep two wives,
1130 nor should the law consent to it.
   Eliduc made her a promise
   and graciously gave her leave:
   he would do what she desired,
   he would give her land.
1135 Near the castle, in the woods,
   at the chapel of the hermitage,
   he had her place her church,
   and build her houses;
   he put much land and wealth into it:
1140 she would have whatever she needed.
   When everything was well prepared,

the lady took the veil
and thirty nuns with her;
she established a rule of life for herself and her order.

1145 Eliduc took his love;
with great honor and a lovely service
the feast was celebrated
on the day he married her.
They lived together many days;
1150 there was perfect love between them.
They gave great alms and did great good,
so much so that they turned to God.
Near the castle, on the other side,
after great care and deliberation
1155 Eliduc founded a church
to which he gave most of his land
and all his gold and silver.
To maintain the order and the house,
he placed his men in it, and other people
1160 devout in their religion.
When he had prepared everything,
he delayed no longer;
with the others he gave and rendered himself up
to serve almighty God.
1165 With his first wife
he placed the wife whom he so cherished.
She received her as her sister
and gave her great honor;
she encouraged her to serve God
1170 and instructed her in her order.
They prayed to God for their friend—
that He would have mercy on him—
and he prayed for them.
He sent messages to them
1175 to find out how they were,
how each was doing.
Each one took great pains

to love God in good faith
and they made a very good end,
1180 thanks to God, the divine truth.

From the adventure of these three,
the ancient courtly Bretons
composed the *lai,* to remember it,
so that no one would forget it.

❦ ELIDUC

ELIDUC, by far the longest of Marie's *lais,* is a more complex
story than it may appear. It brings together the various human
emotions of selfless affection, loyalty, romantic love, desire, self-
indulgence; the bonds between a man and his wife, a man and
his love, and a man and his lord. The only love that can resolve
the conflicts between the others is the love of God, and that
is the solution offered in this, the last *lai.* The story tells of a
man caught between two women, his wife and his new love,
and two lords, the old one who exiles him but to whom he
always feels bound, and the new one, who takes him in. Such
a conflict of loyalties often occurs in medieval romance (see
Tristan, Horn, Ille et Galeron, Li Biaus Desconneus), where it
usually indicates a problem in the man—uncertainty about
himself or about his love, an inability to commit himself en-
tirely or to deny himself anything, an internal conflict exter-
nalized. *Eliduc* is related to at least two of these romances: it
probably influenced the author of *Ille* and was itself influenced
by *Tristan* (most likely the version by Thomas). The differ-
ences between Marie's treatment and the other two tell us a
number of things about Marie's intentions.

In *Ille et Galeron* the hero leaves his first wife because he
thinks he is not worthy of her and he cannot believe in her
love. He becomes involved with the second woman when he

defends her land, but then he encounters his wife again in circumstances that permit no doubts of her love for him. He would rather return to her, but he is now committed to the other woman, and he spends most of the remaining story torn between the two until his wife becomes a nun, leaving him free to marry the other woman and discharge his obligation to her. One is left with the distinct feeling that the first woman is his real love, but that he cannot hold her because of his own failure to trust her love. The author of *Ille,* Gautier d'Arras, retains the basic story line of the *Eliduc* plot, but changes the hero's preference and keeps us more sympathetic to the hero. In *Eliduc,* the hero prefers the new love but the audience sees how superior his wife is, and must feel not only that he has made the wrong decision but that he does not, in fact, deserve his wife.

We see this even more clearly in Marie's treatment of the Tristan material. She reverses the Tristan situation in order to show that Eliduc has made the wrong choice. We know, from the previous *lai, Chevrefoil,* that Marie thinks of the Tristan-Isolt love as a nearly perfect communion, so we can assume that she applauds Tristan's loyalty to his first love, the queen. Marie borrows much of the plot line from Tristan: the hero's exile from his lord, his journey to find adventure and serve other lords (Eliduc's journey, like his loves, is the reverse of Tristan's, moving from Brittany to England), winning the love of the daughter of the lord he serves, their exchange of gifts, his tacit encouragement of her affection by not actively discouraging it, and his secret return to his love (the first Isolt). Eliduc's daily visits to the body of his love in a chapel in the woods recall Tristan's visits to the statue of Isolt in the Hall of Statues, located in a cave in the woods; the chapel which had housed a religious man, a hermit, may also recall the visits to the hermit during the forest exile in Béroul's *Tristan,* but with a significant difference: the hermit recalled Tristan and Isolt to their duty and tried to persuade them to renounce their sin. The main difference between Tristan and Eliduc is that

Tristan, despite his marriage to the second Isolt, which is never consummated, remains loyal to the queen. His affections never swerve from the woman who deserves his loyalty. Even his dalliance with the other woman is occasioned by his love for the queen—he tries unsuccessfully to make himself forget his love by concentrating on another woman, and he pays for that attempt with his death. Here, too, the contrast is significant: Tristan's wife betrays him out of jealousy, while Eliduc's wife spies in order to help her husband; she restores her rival to life and removes herself in order to make way for her. Marie's emphasis is on the selflessness and generosity of real love. It may be to call attention to the significant differences between the two stories that Marie tells us that the name of the *lai* was changed from *Eliduc,* the hero's name, to *Guildeluec and Gualadun,* the names of two women.

Comparison with related stories indicates that Marie does not approve of her hero's actions, but there are similar indications within the story. The first thing we learn about Eliduc is calculated to win our sympathy; he is exiled by his lord through the envy and slander of other barons, punished like Lanval for something he did not do. And yet his behavior through the rest of the *lai* suggests that he is capable of the kind of action for which he is punished, without perhaps even recognizing himself that what he does is wrong. Marie slowly reveals the defects of her hero. His first military exploit is an ambush in which he takes the unarmed enemy unawares, an effective maneuver, but scarcely heroic. When the princess, who is impressed with his exploits, summons him, he hesitates at first to go in to her, but then stays a long time with her. After he has met her, he regrets the long time he has been in that land without knowing her—that is, he resents what he has missed—and only then does he remember that he had promised to be faithful to his wife. Later, when he has received gifts from the princess, he begins to feel himself ill used because he had made that promise. He continues to encourage the girl's affection for him, doing everything short of sleeping with her:

"he couldn't keep himself / from loving the girl . . . from seeing and addressing, / kissing and embracing her" (l. 468 ff.) and the gifts he receives from the girl, the ring and belt, are highly suggestive and certainly signify to her a promise of that kind of love. He refrains only from the final act and thinks that by doing so he remains faithful to his wife and to his new lord, the girl's father. He observes the letter but not the spirit of his vow. The same is true of his loyalty to her father: he will not abduct the girl during his specified term of service, but once that term is over, he feels free to carry her off, even though he cannot hope to marry her. But he does not hesitate to bind himself to her by a set of pledges which must conflict at least in spirit with his marriage vows. Forced by the demands of his first lord to return home, he actually lies to his wife in order to leave her again, telling her the lord he served in the land of his exile still needs him. And finally, when he brings the girl back home with him, endangering the lives of all who accompany him—his sinful act occasions the storm at sea—he murders the sailor who speaks the truth.[1] Thus he betrays the trust of both the women who love him, and there is even some question about his relations with his two lords. He remains loyal to the first lord, despite the unfair treatment, but betrays the second lord by stealing his daughter, although this lord had always treated him well. Perhaps, in some way, his behavior to the second justifies the way the first behaved toward him. Eliduc's loyalty, like his love, is misplaced.

In contrast to the hero's actions, the women never fail in their devotion. The young girl loves purely; she is unable to accept a life of sin and remains unconscious until she is revived by the wife and given the means to regularize her position. The wife behaves with perfect loyalty, generosity, and charity. She is never jealous or vindictive. Hers is an ideal love, which turns finally to God, as it must, since no human object can properly deserve it. And her example leads even the others eventually to turn to God. They end their lives sharing a religious vocation, communicating by letter and praying for each other, rather like Abélard and Héloïse, perhaps the only possible solution in life (death resolves Tristan's conflict) to the problems of secular love.

1. H. S. Robertson suggests that Eliduc tries to operate in a sphere of total unreality, trying to preserve his love in isolation. The sailor's accusation is a brutal intrusion of reality, revealing the extent of Eliduc's trespass into the other world. ("Love and the Other World in Marie de France's 'Eliduc,' " in *Essays in Honor of Louis Francis Solano,* eds. R. J. Cormier and U. T. Holmes, 174.)

❧ SELECTIVE BIBLIOGRAPHY

The following list of editions and secondary materials is far from complete. (Fuller bibliographies can be found in Ewert's edition and in Mickel's book-length study, the latter with annotations.) We include here those works we have found particularly useful, as well as some that are generally considered important for the study of the *Lais*.

EDITIONS

Marie de France, *Lais*. Ed. A. Ewert. Oxford, 1947, repr. 1965.
Les lais de Marie de France. Ed. J. Rychner. Paris, 1969.
Die Lais der Marie de France. Ed. K. Warnke. Halle, 1925.
Die Fablen der Marie de France. Ed. K. Warnke. Halle, 1898.
Marie de France, *Fables* (selected). Eds. A. Ewert and R. C. Johnston. Oxford, 1942.
Das Buch vom Espurgatoire S. Patrice der Marie de France und seine Quelle. Ed. K. Warnke. Halle, 1938.
Marie de France, *L'Espurgatoire Saint Patriz*. Ed. T. A. Jenkins. Chicago, 1903.

SCHOLARLY AND CRITICAL STUDIES

A. Ahlström. *Marie de France et les lais narratifs*. Göteborg, 1925.
H. Baader. *Die Lais. Zur Geschichte einer Gattung der altfranzösischen Kurzerzählungen*. Frankfurt, 1966.
R. Baum. *Recherches sur les oeuvres attribuées à Marie de France*. Heidelberg, 1968.
J. Bédier. "Les lais de Marie de France." *Revue des deux mondes* 107 (1891), 835–63.
G. Brereton. "A 13th Century List of French Lays and Other Narrative Poems." *Modern Language Review* 45 (1950), 40–45.
K. Brightenback. "Remarks on the 'Prologue' to Marie de France's *Lais*." *Romance Philology* 30 (1976), 168–77.
R. Bromwich. "A Note on the Breton Lays." *Medium Aevum* 26 (1957), 36–38.
E. Brugger. "Eigennamen in den *Lais* der Marie de France."

Zeitschrift für französische Sprache und Literatur 49 (1927), 201–52, 381–484.

C. Bullock-Davies. "The Love Messenger in 'Milun.'" *Nottingham Medieval Studies* 16 (1972), 20–27.

R. Cargo. "Marie de France's 'Le Laüstic' and Ovid's *Metamorphoses.*" *Comparative Literature* 18 (1966), 162–66.

R. D. Cottrell. " 'Le lai du Laüstic': From Physicality to Spirituality." *Philological Quarterly* 47 (1968), 499–505.

S. F. Damon. "Marie de France, Psychologist of Courtly Love." *PMLA* 44 (1929), 968–96.

M. Delbouille. "Le nom et le personage d'Equitan." *Le Moyen Age* 69 (1963), 315–23.

M. H. Ferguson. "Folklore in the *Lais* of Marie de France." *Romanic Review* 57 (1966), 3–24.

B. E. Fitz. "The Prologue to the *Lais* of Marie de France and the *Parable of the Talents* and Monetary Metaphor." *Modern Language Notes* 90 (1975), 558–64.

P. N. Flum. "Additional Thoughts on Marie de France." *Romance Notes* 3 (1961), 53–56.

L. Foulet. "Marie de France et les lais bretons." *Zeitschrift für romanische Philologie* 29 (1905), 19–56, 293–322.

J. C. Fox. "Marie de France." *English Historical Review* 25 (1910), 303–6.

———. "Mary Abbess of Shaftesbury." *English Historical Review* 26 (1911), 317–26.

E. A. Francis. "Marie de France et son temps." *Romania* 72 (1951), 78–99.

———. "The Trial in 'Lanval,'" in *Studies . . . Presented to M. K. Pope.* Manchester, 1939, 115–24.

———. "A Commentary on Chevrefoil," in *Medieval Miscellany Presented to Eugene Vinaver.* Manchester, 1965, 136–45.

J. Frappier. "Remarques sur la structure du lai, essai de définition et de classement," in *La litterature narrative d' imagination.* Paris, 1961, 23–39.

J. A. Frey. "Linguistic and Psychological Couplings in the Lays of Marie de France." *Studies in Philology* 61 (1964), 3–18.

R. B. Green. "The Fusion of Magic and Realism in Two Lays of Marie de France." *Neophilologus* 59 (1975), 324–36.

F. Hodgson. "Alienation and the Otherworld in *Lanval, Yonec,* and *Guigemar.*" *Comitatus* 5 (1974), 19–31.

E. Hoepffner. "Pour la chronologie des *Lais* de Marie de France." *Romania* 59 (1933), 351–70; 60 (1934), 36–66.

―――. "La tradition manuscrite des lais de Marie de France." *Neophilologus* 12 (1927), 1–10, 85–96.

―――. "Marie de France et les lais anonymes." *Studi Medievali* 4 (1931), 1–31.

―――. *Les Lais de Marie de France*. Paris, 1935.

―――. "Le geographie et l'histoire dans les lais de Marie de France." *Romania* 56 (1930), 1–32.

U. T. Holmes. "New Thoughts on Marie de France." *Studies in Philology* 29 (1932), 1–10.

R. N. Illingworth. "La chronologie les *Lais* de Marie de France." *Romania* 87 (1966), 433–75.

A. Knapton. "A la recherche de Marie de France." Paper read to the Courtly Literature Society seminar, Modern Language Association meeting, San Francisco, December 1975.

―――. "La Poésie enluminée de Marie de France." *Romance Philology* 30 (1976), 177–87.

M. Lazar. *Amour courtois et "fin'amours" dans la littérature du XIIe siècle*. Paris, 1964.

E. Levi. "Il Re Giovane e Maria di Francia." *Archivum Romanicum* 5 (1921), 448–71.

―――. "Maria di Francia e le abbazie d'Inghilterra." *Archivum Romanicum* 5 (1921), 472–93.

―――. "Sulla cronologia delle opere di Maria di Francia." *Nuovi Studi Medievali* 1 (1923), 40–72.

C. Martineau-Génieys. "Du 'Chievrefoil,' encore et toujours." *Le Moyen Age* 78 (1972), 91–114.

E. J. Mickel. "A Reconsideration of the *Lais* of Marie de France." *Speculum* 46 (1971), 39–65.

―――. "Marie de France's Use of Irony as a Stylistic and Narrative Device." *Studies in Philology* 71 (1974), 265–90.

―――. "The Unity and Significance of Marie's Prologue." *Romania* 95 (1974), 83–91.

―――. *Marie de France*. New York, 1974.

S. Painter. "To Whom were Dedicated the Fables of Marie de France?" *Modern Language Notes* 48 (1933), 367–69.

D. W. Robertson. "Marie de France, *Lais*, Prologue 13–15." *Modern Language Notes* 64 (1949), 336–38.

———. "Love Conventions in Marie's *Equitan*." *Romanic Review* 44 (1953), 241–45.

H. S. Robertson. "Love and the Other World in Marie de France's 'Eliduc,'" in *Essays in Honor of Louis Francis Solano*. Chapel Hill, 1969, 167–76.

F. Schürr. "Komposition und Symbolik in den Lais der Marie de France." *Zeitschrift für romanische Philologie* 50 (1930), 556–82.

C. Segre, "Per l'edizione critica dei *lai* di Maria di Francia." *Culture Neolatina* 19 (1959), 215–37.

L. Spitzer. "Marie de France, Dichterin von Problem-Märchen." *Zeitschrift für romanische Philologie* 50 (1930), 29–67.

———. "The Prologue to the *Lais* of Marie de France and Medieval Poetics." *Modern Philology* 41 (1943), 96–102.

J. Stevens. "The *granz biens* of Marie de France," in *Patterns of Love and Courtesy*, ed. J. Lawlor. Evanston, 1966, 1–25.

K. Warnke. "Über die Zeit der Marie de France." *Zeitschrift für romanische Philologie* 4 (1880), 223–48.

J. Wathelet-Willem. "Equitan dans l'oeuvre de Marie de France." *Le Moyen Âge* 69 (1963), 325–45.

R. D. Whichard. "A Note on the Identity of Marie de France," in *Romance Studies in Honor of W. M. Dey*. Chapel Hill, 1950, 177–81.

B. Wind. "L'idéologie courtoise dans les lais de Marie de France," in *Mélanges . . . Delbouille*, Vol. 2. Gembloux, 1964, 741–48.

E. Winkler. *Marie de France*. Vienna, 1918.

W. Woods. "Marie de France's 'Laüstic.'" *Romance Notes* 12 (1970), 203–7.

For a more thorough bibliography see:

Glyn S. Burgess. *Marie de France: An Analytical Bibliography*. London, 1977.